365 DAYS TO DECL
ORGANIZE YOUR HOME

Written by: Jamie Stewart

Copyright © 2016

All Rights Reserved

Warning-Disclaimer

Table Of Contents

ENTRYWAY   8

KITCHEN   25

BATHROOM 66

DINING ROOM   85

BEDROOM   96

LIVING ROOM   137

CHILDREN'S ROOM 163

PETS   193

LAUNDRY ROOM   199

GARAGE   212

365 DAYS TO DECLUTTER AND ORGANIZE YOUR HOME

If you are tired of seeing the clutter in your house and wasting time looking for items, it's time to tackle the problem once and for all. When your home is jammed with stuff, you might feel a discomfort and pressure.

There is no doubt, clutter can really influence the way you live and work. Your clutter defines a part of you as a person, too. For example, if you love collectibles, these things reflect your passion. If your space is jammed with book clutter, it reveals your personality. However, do not settle with living in a messy home. You deserve better! Consequently, your question is "Where do I start?"

We all know how annoying clutter can be. For people who are overwhelmed by different types of clutter, this may seem like a daunting and never-ending task. Honestly, who has time and energy to declutter the entire house in one go? Luckily, the solution is easier than you suppose. A good decluttering plan and the right tools are just what you need now. There are simple life hacks for decluttering your entire house that will save you time and energy.

Set the mood with your favorite music and get to work! Try to break down the job into a few small manageable tasks and avoid discouragement and tiredness. Divide your entire house into a few zones like this:

a. entryway,

b. kitchen,

c. bathroom

d. living room,

e. dining room,

f. bedroom,

g. children's room,

h. pet area,

i. laundry room,

j. garage.

Next, divide these areas into smaller parts. It could be one shelf, one closet, a wall, and so on.

As you probably already know, it's easy to let our house turn chaotic. Stick to simple rules to streamline your living space. It will be easy because the same basic rules for decluttering work for any room.

Now, focus on one area at a time. Each and every item should fit into one of these zones. If you find some items that don't fit into one of these designated "zones", consider donating or tossing them. It's just that simple!

There is an old adage: "It is better to take many small steps in the right direction than to make a great leap forward only to stumble backward."

This book contains 365 simple and quick decluttering tasks that you can handle easily and effortlessly. Everything big and meaningful starts with baby steps. Here are a few declutter guidelines to help you stay on track.

a. Schedule a decluttering day;

b. Take small simple steps to reach your goal. Start with just fifteen minutes each day. Once you've gotten a part of your house decluttered, take the time to celebrate your small win and enjoy this uncluttered look. Remember – each small win is an accomplishment unto itself.

c. Keep moving. Take another fifteen minutes the next day. And so on. Before you know it, you will have uncluttered and organized a whole room!

Close your eyes and spend a few minutes visualizing your uncluttered home. Think about how you want your home to look. Don't limit yourself and let your imagination run wild! Here are a few smart strategies for you.

- Get essential decluttering tools ready. These are trash boxes and bags, donate boxes and the right organizers.

- Find the right organizers like boxes, tote bags, hutches, and the other appropriate containers. Sort and declutter through your home: then, go out and buy a storage piece.

- Consider buying double-duty furniture pieces.

- Here's a great trick. Take a picture of your room. Then, move just one or two items. Take a picture again. What does it look like? Better?

- Don't force and rush yourself. You can create a "maybe" box if you are not sure. There is a time for everything, so take a deep breath. It's completely normal to feel down sometimes. However, it's important to make progress, a little bit every day. Be a student of life!

You can start clearing and decluttering your entryway. For example, pick a part of your mudroom closet. It doesn't matter what part of the closet. It could be just one shelf. Toss unwanted things and leave the shelf looking neatly organized. Find a place for your essentials. Display your favorites. Then, keep moving. Choose the another room and repeat the same procedure. Take your time to enjoy the new look. Tomorrow is a new day!

A beautiful, uncluttered and well-organized home is the result of the work of all household members. However, if you live with those who do not want to work together, it would be difficult to manage. Then, if you live with a pack-rat, the situation could become even worse. You want to make changes and get organized and they do not want it at all. You tend to organize a simple lifestyle, but they gather things and spend a lot of money. And you can face a terrible mess! Luckily, every problem has a solution!

Have an honest conversation with your family members or roommate. Try to understand their needs, try to be encouraging rather than nagging and negative. Do not judge and stop trying to convince someone to do her/his household chore. Set the standard, but do not tell people how to live their lives. Don't be afraid to express your feelings and show by example – it is the most effective way to get others to follow you. Teach them to love uncluttered house!

"If you would convince a man that he does wrong, do right. But do not care to convince him. Men will believe what they see. Let them see." — Henry David Thoreau

And they will see very quickly – they spend less time cleaning and maintaining things! Remember – nobody's perfect.

Teach your child that he/she doesn't need stuff to be happy. Your children learn by the "monkey see, monkey do" method. So you have to set a good example and find a creative and fun way to involve your kids in the process.

Step into a wonderful world of freedom and beauty hiding behind all that mess!

ENTRYWAY

Entryway makeover

Your entryway is the first place that guests see when they enter your house. There are perfect solutions that can make an efficient entry area. Learn to love the uncluttered look of your entryway. Life is beautiful when you have simple tricks up your sleeve!

1. Use it or lose it!

There is an old American adage "A place for everything and everything in its place". This is so true. The key is to establish a storage spot for every single object in your entryway. Simplify your life. Determine the essentials and find them their home. Clean the clutter out of your entryway once and for all. This rule applies to all rooms without exception. Even for the basement and attic.

2. Consider adding mudroom.

Do you have a hall closet jammed with clutter? Here are a few life hacks for decluttering and cleaning out your hall closet.

a. While you are going through this mess, ask yourself: Do I really need all these things in my hall closet? Is anything in this area unused? Toss unwanted items. You can donate some of them to a homeless shelter.

b. Anyway, if you have a lot of items and you can't get rid of them, consider adding a mudroom.

The overburdened hall closet is something quite normal for most families. However, you can conquer your hall closet.

If you are able, you can build a small room around your front door. It could have walls of glass with charming shelves for potted plants. So you will spend less time cleaning and maintaining things.

3. Mudroom organizing idea: Table with drawers.

Your mudroom can be one of the most challenging rooms to keep organized. All year round. You and your kids bring lots of junk home. Umbrellas, shopping bags, briefcases, newspapers, all of these items have a way of getting dumped in the entryway. Don't let your entry room become a chaotic place. You can equip your mudroom with lockers, floating shelves, bins, baskets for outdoor toys, etc.

Consider buying a nice table with a drawers and shelf underneath. So, you can place large items upon the shelf, while smaller things, like keys or papers, can go in the drawers.

4. Remove off-season items and hide clutter instantly!

There is an old space-saving idea – remove off-season items from your entryway. Don't store them in your hall closet. It's summertime and you still keep kids' ski equipment in your entryway closet. Remove these items to another convenient place (e.g. basement, attic, garage etc.)

You should also consider buying an attractive bureau (a chest of drawers) to hide unwanted items instantly. However, designate a spot for keys, a spot for sunglasses, wallets, etc. And stick to it.

5. Multipurpose rooms that work.

You can also merge the mudroom function with the functions of a kitchen storage by adding cupboards, drawers, and even a small freezer. At the same time, you will declutter your kitchen and pantry. You can also create mudroom/laundry room by putting your washer there. The possibilities are endless. Lovely!

6. Solutions for non-existent entryway.

The front entry forms the first impression. No entry hall? No worries, there are perfect solutions that can make an efficient entry area.

a. A pile of shoes, baskets, boxes, kids' backpacks... There are too many items at the entrance of your home. Get rid of unwanted things that are located at your front door.

b. Try your best to create a functional walkway.

c. Work vertically and use any small bits of wall.

d. Opt for the right furniture. Choose consoles with a narrow profile or folding chairs.

e. Make your items work double-duty. For instance, you can use a storage bench.

7. Define your entry with this clever idea.

You can create the illusion of an entryway by using a small-sized bookshelf as a room divider. Everything from mail and school papers to backpacks and caps can find a spot in a hutch like this. You can put a basket for keys, a tray for small items and other items here.

A shallow bookshelf will separate your entry from the rest of your house. It will define the entry area while taking up very little space.

8. Life hack – mudroom cubby systems!

Mudroom cubbies can bring order to all these accessories you and your family use on a daily basis. A lot of items such as toys, shopping bags, boxes newspapers, flip-flops, backpacks, handbags have a way of getting dumped around your doorway.

If you prefer more hidden storage, don't use open cubbies. You should install cubbies with doors. Then, pay attention to the size of your cubbies. You don't want those cubbies take up most of space in your mudroom. This great and useful piece of furniture helps keep your entryway clutter-free.

And remember – your foyer is the first place that guests see when they enter your house. Choose some chic mudroom cubbies and make a great first impression!

9. Remember to organize your shoes.

There is no doubt that even a few pairs of extra shoes can create mess and clutter. How to declutter your shoes? There are a few basic tips:

a. Therefore, the standard tip is simple – get rid of anything you have not worn in a year or two. You can donate your old shoes.

b. You may be able to repair some pair of shoes.

c. Everything else that you can't wear or donate, just throw it in the trash.

d. A simple pallet can be used to store shoes. Remove off-season shoes from your entryway.

It's important to maintain this new clutter-free environment you've created. Once a month, you should take some time to clean this space of dust and dirt. And remember – it gets easier with time!

10. Declutter your shoes – a simple shoe bench.

Do you have the pile of shoes and boots that have accumulated by your door? What could you do with this clutter?

Consider buying a simple shoe bench. Each family member can be assigned a place for holding their shoes.

Place a mat inside the door and clean it frequently. Ask all family members to put their shoes on their designated spots.

11. Savvy shoe storage ideas.

You have a lot of shoes, right? Rain boots, shoes for play, sneakers, slippers, sandals, etc. To keep your shoes protected and well organized, you should find the right organizer.

Here are a few storage ideas to keep your footwear neat and tidy.

a. **Shoe storage cabinet** is one of the best solutions for your entryway. For sure, you have to have a space that is large enough for it.

b. **Shoe rack** is a handy and cut solution.

c. **Hanging storage** fits perfectly on your door.

d. **Floor to ceiling shelf** is an amazing solution for small apartments.

You should purchase a proper shoe organizer according to your personal needs and preferences. The choice is yours.

12. Creative and unusual shoe storage ideas.

Your footwear collection can make your home looks cluttered. Fortunately, there are many cheap and simple ideas. Looking for inspiration? These ideas work for all types of apartments and houses, especially for small apartments.

a. **Hooks.** You can hang shoes on hooks or nails. Therefore, your shoes will be right at hand.

b. **Convenient shelves**. Consider installing wall mounted shelves. From now on, you can organize your shoes without taking up any floor space at all.

c. **Stylish towel rod**. You can hang your high heels on the towel rod. It is a great minimal look!

d. **Cart.** You can fit all of your slippers into a slim cart to wheel around the entryway.

13. Pant hangers and crown molding for your shoes.

Here are two great ideas to organize your shoes.

a. Hang your tall boots on pant hangers in your closet and save a lot of space on the closet floor.

b. Use crown molding to organize your high heels. You just have to attach them to the wall upside down. So, free up the floor space and get your favorite shoes well organized.

14. A clever way to organize high heels.

"I don't know who invented high heels, but all women owe him a lot." – Marilyn Monroe.

Ladies are aware that even a few pairs of high heels can create clutter. This is because you didn't find a spot for them all. Nonetheless, ladies are constantly buying new shoes, particularly high heels.

Don't worry at all, there are creative ways to organize your high heels in a closet, even in your entryway. You can purchase tall shoe box in a size that perfectly fits your favorite high heels. You will protect your shoes from potential wear-and-tear. This is just one of the hundreds of possibilities. If you get inspired, you can tackle this task as well.

15. Declutter grimy winter footwear in your entryway.

Grimy shoes are scattered all over your hallway. Place a boot tray next to the front door.

You can find them at local home improvement superstore. You can go the extra mile for your family by putting wheels on the tray. It makes stylish boot statement.

For that purpose, you can also design a rolling shoe crate.

16. Time-saving solutions for mudroom closet.

You're probably spending too much time decluttering and cleaning your hallway, as well as every other room in your house. However, there are time-saving solutions. In order to do that, you need to start by changing your decluttering approach.

    a. **Get a jump start on your mudroom closet.** As you work through the items in your mudroom closet, here are two important questions to keep in mind: Is this useful? Is this beautiful? Now throw out any clutter that are laying around.

b. **Decide on the purpose.** Ask yourself: What is the function of this closet? For instance, if you don't have a coat closet, so coats can go there. If you're lacking wardrobe space, you can install a cute holder with clothespins to hang hats, caps, gloves, etc.

c. **Maximize space.** This is definitely an area where closet is a big help. You can choose long narrow closet to maximize space in your entryway. However, it all depends on the space that is available to you. You are ready to start living your life!

17. Organize a small entryway closet – Closet makeover.

You can organize all items in your small entry closet with a few clever ideas. Here are a few pointers for cleaning out your small entry closet.

a. First of all, free up your space. Empty your closet and bring all items together. Make sure that you are sorting items into designated piles: things to throw away, things to donate, and things to sell. After that, reorganize your items.

b. Then, consider using vertical space in your closet. There are amazing vertical shoe organizers that will hold 20 pairs of shoes and more.

18. A space-saving idea for your small entryway closet.

There is a brilliant idea to maximize closet space. Tiny hangers are perfect items for your tiny entryway. There is a variety of materials and brands, so give it a try.

Of course, this isn't a permanent solution. You'll have to take time to declutter your small closet occasionally. You'll be able to simplify the clutter so that you can enjoy your closet to the fullest. Learn to love the uncluttered look of your entryway!

19. Take the entryway organization to the next level.

Do you have coat stand that is cluttered with coats, jackets, gloves, and scarves? And your coat stand takes too much space, right?

a. Declutter your coat stand. Get rid of excess items. Donate some of your coats and jackets to charity.

b. A row of wall pegs can be a great asset.

c. Then, you can use clothespins that have a hook for wet mittens or gardening gloves. These hooks can be found at a local hardware store or home centers.

20. The wire baskets for simple organization.

If your entryway space isn't big enough for a furniture, use wire baskets to keep clutter out of sight. They will make it easy for you to store your sports equipment like balls, bike helmets, mittens, and other everyday items. It would be great if you are able to invest in baskets with lids.

21. Gym lockers for your small mudroom.

You don't have to buy a mudroom cabinet. Here is a clever idea to maintain your clutter-free environment. Gym lockers make very useful storage options for the mudroom. Try to find vintage gym lockers online; then, prime and paint them to match your mudroom. They are tall and narrow so that they are ideal for a small place. Each family member will be assigned a locker for holding coats, shoes, umbrella, backpack or other things.

22. Reorganize your keys.

Every family member has a bunch of keys. Are they scattered everywhere?

Organize your keys in a designated spot in your entryway. You can use a bowl or rack.

23. A decluttering secret from professional organizers.

You can utilize your entryway to put a trash bin. Your family and guests can empty their pockets or purses there. In this way, they don't bring any trash to your house. Teach your kids to use that trash bin, so this simple hack will make a big difference.

24. Use stylish wrought iron hooks.

Do you want to have some everyday items at your fingertips? You can use some pretty wrought iron hooks to hold seasonal jackets, pet leashes, bags, baskets with handles, and other things. Life is beautiful when you have simple tricks up your sleeve! You can also hang the basket to hold small items such as keys or papers. Each family member will be assigned a couple of hooks for holding seasonal and everyday items. Lovely!

25. Keep your screws and nuts in one place with this clever idea.

Every home has some extra bolts, nails, nuts, and screws, and they can easily get lost. Putting them away is easy, but finding them is the hard part.

You can store them in between packing tape. Next, label it with a permanent marker. Perfect! Put these packs in a designated drawer. The little things make us happy, right? Catch clutter and reorganize your home and your life!

26. Sports equipment and outdoor toys.

Kids' items for outdoor activities are usually scattered in your entryway. You can use a trash can for these items, but there are a lot of advanced ideas.

a. Use duffel bags for sports equipment. Tote bags are also a great idea.

b. Hang up tennis rackets on the walls. There are other items that can be hung on hooks on the wall, too. Let your imagination run wild!

c. You can designate a spot for each of sports activity. Kids' bins are perfect solutions for these items.

d. For small items that tend to get thrown around you can use an old bookshelf.

27. Too many baskets.

A basket is a clever solution for almost all kinds of things. Toys, spray bottles, beauty products, and so on. Baskets are great for a quick fix, too. Especially if you are not ready for unexpected guests or you are in a hurry. In this way, you can teach kids to pick up after themselves.

You can make some way to use up that big gap of space under your entryway cabinet. You can also use some cup hanger hooks to hang your baskets with handles. It will make a big difference. Give it a try!

28. Keep incoming/outgoing mail organized in your entryway.

There are too many paperwork, mail, school papers, and the other paper that you get each day. Where do you put them? If you put them into your entryway every day, you might as well have a designated spot for them.

    a. Bring all papers together and check them out. Toss every unwanted paper.

    b. Try to use each and every nook in your entryway. Keep your incoming/outgoing mail organized and tidy in a latter cage. Simply hang a small cage on the wall and use vertical space. Lovely!

29. Another way to organize incoming/outgoing mail.

Where do your papers go when you walk in the door? Keep everything in one easy-to-find place like a bill clips. Mount a few bill clips on a wall in your hallway to keep track of your paperwork.

30. Dealing with your kids.

When your kids arrive home from school, they like to dump their backpacks somewhere in a hallway. Backpacks, jackets, caps, and school supplies can get scattered next to the front door. It will create a lot of clutter, right?

To help your kids to build a good habit of putting away their stuff, use this little trick. Place wall hooks at convenient spots by the door for their backpacks. If your kids can't reach the coat rack, assign wall hooks for their coats, jackets, scarves and so on.

31. Let your imagination run wild!

If you have been decluttering for the past few days, you certainly got tired. Wait a minute. You already take your first step. This advice will help you not to give up – Change your perspective and use your imagination!

For instance, take photos of your house. You will see your home in a completely new light! You can only take a picture of the room you have already organized. It will give you an extra incentive. Remove just one or two things more. Take picture again. Isn't it better? Well done! Just keep up the good work!

KITCHEN

Hello kitchen!

It's time to tackle the kitchen clutter. You should divide your kitchen into several main zones:

- food;

- cooking, baking, and food preparation;

- cleaning;

- storage;

Therefore, every item in your kitchen should fit into one of these four groups. Thus, you can declutter, organize and clean entire kitchen easily and effortlessly. Maybe you think you can't make time to remove trash from your kitchen, but there is a simple solution. Just focus on one small area, one by one!

32. There is no wrong place to start.

"Do not wait; the time will never be just right. Start where you stand, and work with whatever tools you may have at your command, and better tools will be found as you go along." – Napoleon Hill

Therefore, focus on the part of your kitchen. That might be one drawer, it doesn't matter. It does not sound just like a revolutionary idea, but you will build one small success on top of another small success. Afterwards, you can build a "mountain" of success.

    a. Examine the selected drawer. Then, empty the drawer on the kitchen table on a counter.

    b. Immediately get rid of what you won't need. Do not accumulate anything, and put unnecessary items into donation boxes and garbage bags.

    c. Then, clean the drawer, and sort the items by frequency of use. Purchase drawer dividers and organize everything. Arrange things that are used the most frequently in the front part of the drawer. Put rest of the thing behind them.

This bright idea will save your time and energy.

33. Reorganize and declutter floating shelves in the kitchen.

Now, you have to declutter floating shelves in the kitchen. The way you organize your shelves also plays a part in making a clean and tidy kitchen.

    a. Place a large quilt on the floor.

    b. Remove items from your floating shelves, one by one and transfer them to the quilt. In this way, you can see an abundance of stuff in your kitchen. You may need to remove some items to the other room.

    c. It's time to clean your items that have gotten dusty.

d. Afterwards, place things back in floating shelves.

And remember – Balance is the key to a happy kitchen. Don't overfill your space with a lot of things. Realistically, how many baking dishes, measuring cups or graters do you need? Get rid of the surplus and take back your kitchen!

34. Declutter small kitchen appliances.

If you have a lot of small appliances, they can create a clutter. Here are a few ideas to take control of your small appliances.

a. Before organizing those items, take inventory. How many small appliances do you have? Have you been given a lot of hand-me-downs?

b. Declutter duplicate appliances. For example, if you have two blenders, think about letting one of them go. You can sell these items at a garage sale or you can donate them to charity.

c. Ask yourself: Which ones do you use most frequently? Divide all items into two categories: "rarely use" and "use often." Therefore, keep only necessary items and purge the rest.

d. Therefore, try to store what you will use. Keep your small appliances well organized in a kitchen cabinet.

Therefore, when you want to find certain appliance, you will always know where it is.

35. A systematically organized cooking space.

You can make the most of your kitchen. Before you start cluttering of your cooking zone, consider how many cabinets you have. Which area are used for which cooking tasks? How many kitchen appliances and dishes can you purge? You can get a detailed plan on paper.

a. Bring all cooking utensils and tools together. Toss unwanted cooking tools.

b. Put the spices, oils and bottles of vinegar into designated spots.

c. Organize spoons, knives, cutting boards, etc.

d. Organize your pots, pans skillets, and other cookware. Try to organize all cookware close to your stove. And from now onwards, when you want to find your cooking tool, you'll always know where it is.

36. Prepare your meals in decluttered kitchen.

Cookware such as mixing bowls, cutting boards, kitchen gadgets, knives and blender should be organized in a specific area. In this way, they will always be at your fingertips. Cut through the unnecessary kitchen tools that might have accumulated. Get rid of items that don't work. Free up space in your kitchen so that you can enjoy your space to the fullest.

37. Create more cook-friendly kitchen.

If you are able, create a station on your counter where you will keep your cooking essentials. Cooking oil, salt, black pepper, and garlic are the most commonly used cooking ingredients. In this way, your space becomes more cook-friendly. Use an old cutting board to designate this spot.

38. Organize your pots and pans.

Empty your kitchen cabinet and utilize it for your pots and pants. Begin with the largest pots so arrange them on the bottom of the cabinet; then, work upwards to the smallest pots and pans. Or store them on an open shelf. Of course, get rid of old and rusty pots and pans and organize the good ones.

Your pans and pots get unwanted stains? Don't waste your time to scrub and clean them. You can utilize this great trick and remove the stains easily and effortlessly. You will need apple peels. Yes, that's it! Strip off pot stains with apple peels.

Add the apple peels to your pan or pot; pour in water; then, allow the water to simmer for about 3 minutes. Then, pour out the water; lastly, cleanse the pot with a rag.

39. Another way to keep pots and pans well organized.

Countertops look like magnets for clutter. Unwashed dishes, utensils, bags, pots, pans, there are too many items there. You can start with all these pots and pans and find a convenient place to store them. Otherwise, you will not be able to cook, bake and eat. If you continue to pile up all these things, your kitchen will be jammed with clutter.

The most common and the easiest way to organize your pots and pans is to hang them on the wall. If you're lacking cabinet space, hang your cookware. Take back your kitchen!

40. Pot and pan holder.

If you do not know what to do with pots and pans because you have a small kitchen, there is no need to be concerned. You can easily build a simple storage area for your favorite cookware.

How about using an old pallet for this purpose? You have to paint the pallet: then, anchor the pallet to the wall with drywall screws; lastly, you should add some hangers. In this way, you can keep your pots and pans neat and tidy.

41. Don't forget to organize and declutter your knives.

There are too many knives in your kitchen. Bring all knives together on a kitchen table. Get rid of unwanted knives. Now you should organize the good ones. It may be hard to get started, but it saves you work. There are a few great ways to keep your knives organized.

a. Hang knives on a magnetic strip.

b. Consider putting your knives in a designated drawer, but make sure to organize them with drawer dividers.

c. In-drawer knife block is also a great solution.

42. Organize your cutting boards.

The old magazine rack is a great storage option. You can install magazine rack inside the cabinet door to hold your cutting boards. You should screw the rack on the inside of cabinet door. This is an amazing space saver and a great spot for easy access to your cutting boards. Nice and tidy!

43. Lazy Susan – Spice organizers.

For those who are overwhelmed by kitchen clutter, here is a great idea to declutter your spices. Do you constantly buy herbs and spices? Do you spend money buying duplicates for spices you already have somewhere? Do you keep expired spices? Your spice rack may be jammed with unwanted bottles of spices and herbs.

Use Lazy Susan as your new spice organizer. You can use multiple Lazy Susans and divide your favorite spices into categories. You can organize everything by grouping items by type and frequency of use. Items that are used the most frequently should be the most accessible. It's important not to limit yourself. Spice it up!

44. Alphabetize your favorite spices.

Have you got a large variety of spices? Do you like cooking and experiment with new flavors? Do you want to keep your herbs and spices organized? It will take only 15 minutes and you will find what you need much easier every time you cook.

To alphabetize your favorite spices, bring them together. First, toss out expired spices. Then, arrange them in alphabetical order. A spice rack will help you to keep them organized once and for all. There is only one rule you should follow – put every spice back into its proper spot after the usage.

45. How to organize your bakeware?

How many pieces of baking equipment do you really need? It depends on the size of your family and your personal preferences. It's not the same thing: bake the cookies for yourself and your spouse or baking for six-member family. Further, if you adore baking and you bake croissants, rolls, cookies, and cakes more frequently, you will need proper baking equipment. On the other hand, if you mainly buy your favorite treats in the bakery, you will need less baking items.

The average kitchen contains many more dishes than it is necessary. In other words, if you think that you need a wide variety of baking items, here's a simple guideline. Four-member family will need:

   a. **Bakeware:** 2-qt baking dish, 1 8x8 casserole, 2 cookie sheets, 2 muffin tins, 1 tart pan, 2 round cake pans, and 1 bread pan.

b. **Baking equipment:** a rolling pin, a wire rack, 2-3 mixing bowls, 1-2 cookie cutters, and flour sifter.

Get rid of unwanted baking items. Throw away everything that is rusty, warped and useless. In this way, you can organize and store your bakeware. It means you should store bakeware and baking equipment in a kitchen cupboard that is near to your oven. The clutter will be gone and you will enjoy baking in the comfort of your home.

46. Create a baking zone.

Do you like making delicious cookies, rolls, loaves of bread and other bakery products? Keeping all of your ingredients within arm's reach of your preparation area will make you feel great. You can corral all ingredients in a designated kitchen cabinet or shelf. Clear out the designated kitchen cabinet and make space for your favorites.

a. Bring all of your baking ingredients together and check the expiration dates.

b. Throw unwanted ingredients away.

c. Create a list of missing ingredients and go shopping as soon as possible.

d. Put the ingredients into containers or mason jars, grouping them according to their purpose.

e. Label these containers and jars and stock your new space.

Enjoy baking and fall in love with the order in your baking zone.

47. How to keep your baking cabinet neat and tidy?

If you make baked goods frequently, you like keeping your ingredients on hand.

- Use large-sized containers for flours, granulated sugar, powdered sugar, and old-fashioned oats.

- Next, medium-sized containers are perfect for brown sugar, chocolate chips, and tapioca.

- Use small-sized containers for cocoa powder, baking powder, baking soda, cornstarch, and coconut.

You can choose any type of containers that easy to open when your hands are messy. Fill your containers with the ingredients and you will tackle this task easily and effortlessly.

48. A kitchen organizing trick for baking sheets.

Are your baking trays and sheets falling all over kitchen shelves and cabinets? Or it's difficult to find the baking tray that you need right now. The reason is that you didn't create a special place for your bakeware and they are scattered with other dishes. Here's a great kitchen organizing trick. Keep your bakeware organized on top of kitchen cupboards! In this way, they are always easily accessible.

49. Reorganize and categorize kitchen utensils.

Your hand-held kitchen tools deserve a special spot in your kitchen. There are so useful and you want to have them at your fingertips. Cheese knife, bread knife, spatulas, colander, corkscrew, filet knife, funnel, grater, lemon squeezer, baster, and other utensils can create a lot of clutter.

a. You can group them together and categorize them by their various uses.

b. Clear out all of your drawers and wipe them down.

c. Then, get rid of utensils that you haven't used in the last year. Try to donate as much as you can.

d. Use baskets, bins and trays for storing your most commonly used utensils.

e. If you're short on space, you can store them in your large-sized slow cooker.

50. Declutter your recipes and cookbooks.

If you set some ground rules, every item falls into its place. One of these ground rules is – you should complete each area before moving on to the next area. Today, decide to organize recipes and cookbooks. If you take your time, turn on the music and make a cup of tea for yourself, it will seem like a breeze.

The whole process depends on how many loose recipes you have got piled up. If you are constantly waste time searching for certain recipes, it's time for decluttering and organizing. Here are a few pointers for organizing your cookbook and recipes.

a.   Bring all recipes and cookbooks together.

b.   Then, think about your reasons for saving recipes. Therefore, review each and every recipe. Get a garbage bag ready. Toss all unwanted recipes and organize all your reams of recipes.

c.   Sort the recipes by categories. Divide them into groups. For example, old family recipes, new non-tested recipes, practical recipes, etc. Whatever you like. Enjoy cooking!

51. Find the right home in your home for your favorite recipes.

The kitchen is the heart of the home. Your kitchen allows you to express your creativity through organizing and cooking. If this space is well-planned and organized, you can enjoy eating, food prep, and cooking.

In terms of cookbooks and recipes, here are a few organizing ideas:

a. Some cookbooks that you use on a regular basis deserve a special spot in the kitchen. As far as the rest of cookbooks, you can arrange them on bookshelf outside the kitchen.

b. Journal type notebooks with bound-in pages.

c. Photo albums with clear plastic protectors.

d. Computer cookbook and recipe software.

52. No pantry solutions.

Do you live in a small house or an apartment without a pantry? Many apartments are pantry-less, no big deal! You still can make the most of your small kitchen.

a. First, get a garbage bag ready and toss the old food and expired items.

b. You can designate a few cupboards in which to store your food.

c. In order to get extra space storage, you can lose the boxes.

d. Use baskets to corral small items.

e. Try to use space in your refrigerator to the fullest.

f. Try to use each and every nook in the kitchen cabinets.

53. Organize food in your pantry.

Another area to declutter will likely be your pantry for sure. The pantry is one of the biggest clutter magnets in every house.

First, check out the labels, and read expiration dates carefully. Then, throw away expired items. Donate foods that you will not plan to eat, the food that no longer fit your dietary regimen or your children no longer want to eat that.

Here are some useful tips for you.

- For instance, designate a shelf for drinks, coffee, and tea.

- Designate an easy to rich area with healthy snacks for your children.

- Organize your cupboards so that the items you use most frequently could be the most accessible.

In this way, you can also teach your kids to always put things back in their designated places.

54. Organize your foods by categories.

Now you can start grouping foods by categories. There are five basic categories:

1) **Canned goods and jars**

2) **Bulk items** (e.g. rice, nuts, beans, and other dry goods)

3) **Snacks**

4) **Chocolate and desserts**

5) **Prepackaged food**

Don't forget to use doors. You should use the space on the inside of your pantry doors. Purchase a good door organizer and store bottles, sauces, jars, etc. And an extra tip for you: Use a pantry inventory sheet and pen to keep track of what you have!

55. Organize your canned goods and jars once and for all.

Every family likes canned goods. Jam, pickled vegetables, salads, yummy! Organizing canned goods and jars in a pantry can be achieved in many different ways. Of course, it depends on your own preferences. This is a handy tip that will save the space in your pantry.

Add a tiered shelf to the pantry to see easily all of your jars. How to choose the right tiered shelves? Here are three major criteria: 1) pay attention to the size of the canned goods you typically store; 2) consider the amounts of your canned goods; 3) pay attention to space available in your kitchen or pantry.

Then, arrange your jars and cans and enjoy. A great option for corralling the various canned goods is to utilize an over-the-door organizer. It's time to take back your pantry!

56. Organize your bulk items and dried goods.

Bean bags, flour, rice, oats, sugar, cereals, lentils, and the other dried goods need their special place. It is true they take up a lot of space, but if they are well organized, you will not have that issue. Dried goods can create a lot of dirt, too. These foods make a lot of crumbs all over the kitchen cabinets. Especially open bags!

   a. First of all, get a supply of glass jars.

   b. Next, check expiration dates and toss expired dried goods.

   c. Sort your food into groups. For example, bring all types of sugar together: powdered sugar, brown sugar, caster sugar, granulated sugar, etc. Put each type of sugar into a separate jar. Add labels for easier orientation. Done!

d. Afterwards, you should follow this rule – put every jar back into its proper spot after the usage. That's it!

57. A shoe organizer can help you to organize all these snacks.

Your family loves snacks, right? However, they are falling on the floor of your pantry, they are chucked to the back end. You are looking for the seasoning packets and you can't find them! There is a simple trick for that. A plastic Over-the-Door shoe organizer is your solution! It is perfect for storing all these bags and boxes.

a. Hang a shoe organizer on the door of the pantry.

b. Put your favorite snacks into their seats.

58. How to store chocolate and desserts – Make sense of the mess.

De-cluttering your pantry will make meal preparation and food shopping much easier.

You should keep these general guidelines in mind:

a. First of all, check expiration dates and toss expired treats. Discard all sweets that have been opened a long time ago.

b. Give away or donate any chocolate or dessert that you won't eat.

c. Store your chocolate away from direct sunlight, protected from moisture.

d. If you store the chocolate in a kitchen cabinet, you can use closet racks as organizers.

59. Organize your tea bags.

It's tea time. Do you have a dozen different types of tea? Do they take up a lot of space? They are scattered in your kitchen closet, right? There is a clever solution to keep them well organized. You should make a tea tin with some dividers. Take a tin container with the lid and put a decorative paper into the bottom of the tin. Measure and cut cardboard in order to make dividers. You can label them if you like. Add tea bags in each compartment. You can use smaller or bigger container, it's up to you. It will free up space in your cabinet.

This method will require you to purchase spice jars, but it's an effective organizational method and should appeal to those who like uniformity. Make sure you measure the height of the jars and drawers before purchasing. You can even go one step further and organize your spice drawer alphabetically. It sounds crazy, but it will make your life easier. If you are switching your spices into new containers, do not forget to label the bottom of the jars with the expiration date.

60. Keep bulk herbal teas neat and tidy.

If you and your family like bulk tea, you probably have a lot of tiny bags in your kitchen. They are scattered all over kitchen cabinet and you waste your time searching for certain herbal tea. And you feel helpless and hopeless. It's time to solve the problem.

Purchase medium-sized screwed jars. This organizational method should appeal to those who like uniformity. You can even go one step further and organize your teas alphabetically. And of course, do not forget to label the jars with the names of your teas and expiration date. Voilà! This will make your life much easier.

61. Clean your stovetop with leftover vegetable oil.

It's time to declutter your oils. If you have leftover cooking oils, oils for salad dressings or for other purposes, don't throw them away. You can use it in a way that you couldn't imagine. You can clean your stovetop without harsh chemicals. Yes, you can!

The grease buildup on the stovetop can be eliminated with leftover vegetable oil. So drop a few dribbles of leftover oil on the grease stain. Then, rub at it with kitchen paper towel. Done!

62. Trays – Organizing idea for your kitchen counter.

First of all – remove the unnecessary things that don't belong here. You should also remove teapots, toasters, coffee makers, and so on. Honestly, if you make coffee only in the morning, it'll take about 5 minutes every day. After that, your coffee maker will stand unused by tomorrow morning.

Take trays of different sizes and shapes that will hold different items. Each of them will have a specific purpose. One tray holds napkins and coasters. The other tray will be "home" for salt, pepper, spices you use frequently, bottles of the oil, etc. The third tray will be home for important things such as keys.

63. Organize your food containers.

Are these great containers for wet or dry foods scattered in your cupboards? Further, you have food containers without their lids and those that are cracked or smelly or stained. Now it is absolutely clear that you should throw them away. Honestly, you probably have too many kippers. You need 4 small rectangular containers for individual serving lunches, 2 large containers for salads, and 2 containers for packing snacks. That's it!

You can put the containers into a cupboard or a large drawer, it's up to you. Then, organize them by size and shape. Begin with the largest containers and place them on the bottom; then, work upwards to the smallest containers.

64. Get rid of that messy pile in your kitchen drawer.

Do you have a junk drawer in your kitchen? While you are going through this pile, ask yourself: Do I really need all these things in my kitchen? You can find markers that have dried out, broken pencils, empty bottles, anything and everything. Of course, they don't belong in the kitchen drawers. Empty the drawer and start cleaning.

Get rid of anything that is almost empty. Sure, there are necessary items that should be stored somewhere else. Therefore, transfer them to the suitable places. When you have finished this dirtiest part of the job, you can organize your drawer.

65. The clever solutions for your junk drawer.

It's time to organize your junk drawer once and for all. The question is: What would you like to have handy but hidden? So grab a few organizers (e.g. recycle sturdy plastic containers) and divide those miscellaneous items into categories. It's clear that you have to go through your junk drawer and tidy up it from time to time. It is important to bring junk under control and maintain organization.

An extra tip: You can use an ice cube tray for small things.

66. Keep your refrigerator clean and organized (Part I).

a. Take a big trash bag.

b. Declutter the outside of your refrigerator (remove notes, children's drawings, fridge magnets, etc.) Do you really need those cheap magnets you received as the promotional items?

c. Remove all drawers and shelves.

d. Get rid of old and expired items from your refrigerator and freezer.

67. Keep your refrigerator clean and organized (Part II).

a. Clean your refrigerator thoroughly. Use mild soap and water.

b. Place washable lining in the drawers and on the shelves. They will absorb spills. Replace them every six months.

c. Add everything back to your refrigerator. Use organizing bins on the shelves. Use containers to keep like items together.

d.   Create your shopping list.

68. Declutter refrigerator shelves and drawers.

It is extremely important to understand the basic rules for organizing the refrigerator. Here are some of them.

a.   Put condiments on the door of the refrigerator.

b.   Meats and cheeses should be kept in the coldest part of your refrigerator.

c.   Take some vegetable bins for the fresh products.

d.   Keep beverages on a designated shelf.

e.   Designate certain shelves for certain items. Therefore, you can find them quickly and easily. Consider labeling the containers to make it easy for your family to put things into their places.

69. Take organization to the next level.

Consider labeling the containers in your refrigerator. Take the organization of your refrigerator to a new level. Put removable labels on many of the containers. It sounds crazy, but it will make your life easier. You will be able to see the entire content of your fridge at a glance.

70. It's time to organize your freezer (Part I).

Having a neat and tidy freezer will save your time, energy, and money. Here are a few pointers for organizing and cleaning out your freezer.

a. Unplug your freezer and remove the ice from the freezer trays.

b. Ditch anything that has expired. Get rid of freezer-burnt food. Toss the food that you will never eat.

c. Clean your freezer thoroughly. Scrub it with a sponge, water, mild soap or homemade cleaner. Clean up the drawers and detachable shelves. Wipe down the walls of your freezer with paper towels.

d. Add drawers, shelves and the food back. Seal your food in food-saver bags.

Put these tips into practice and you will enjoy your frozen food!

71. It's time to organize your freezer (Part II).

a. Group all your food into categories based on how often you use it.

b. It's time to gather up your supplies. Therefore, consider purchasing some organizers. Use at least one bin for each category of food. You can find inexpensive plastic containers to store your food properly. Make sure to choose the right containers, such as adequate foils, plastic bags, or plastic containers. Your goal is to keep air out and maximize freezer space.

c. Actually, you should freeze foods with high moisture content. You should know what's freezable. You can freeze meat, fish, berries, shrimp, etc. On the other hand, you can't freeze fried foods or yogurt.

d. If you want to be even more organized, take the time to label and date your foods. You don't want to defrost the wrong thing, right?

72. Go one step further.

You are doing very well! Keep up the good work! It's time to take the organization on your freezer to the next level.

a. Prevent your freezer burn. From time to time, sort through each container in order to place the oldest items in front of the freezer.

b. If you buy in bulk, you should purchase a deep freezer.

c. Find a creative way to divide up space. Consider buying modern freezer dividers.

73. An unexpected way to use a magazine holder.

Do you like frozen foods? Frozen vegetables, fruits, fish, nuts, etc. But these bags are scattered all over your freezer and it is difficult to find what you need. Have you ever had that painful moment when you open your freezer and some heavy item falls down on your toe? If you had that "ouch" experience, you know that you have to reorganize your freezer.

You can use your old magazine holders to store bagged frozen foods. You can add labels and take your task to the next level. And from now on, when you want to find some frozen food, you will always know where it is. Lovely!

74. Declutter your kitchen gadgets and appliances.

How to know when to throw some gadgets away or donate them to charity? Group these items

into following categories:

- You haven't used it in the last year

- You know for sure that your family will never use it again. Just create" I would never use that" list

- It is too old

- It is broken and completely useless

- You have duplicate

After this, it's easy to know what to do next. Enjoy!

75. Store your kitchen gadgets and appliances.

The best way to keep your kitchen gadgets organized is to group them by type. Otherwise, you will forget what you have and where you put it. Here is an example.

    a. **The first group:** hand mixer, stand mixer, blender, food processor, and juicer.

    b. **The second group:** toaster, panini press, popcorn machine, and waffle iron.

    c. **The third group:** deep fryer, bread machine, pressure cooker, rice cooker, and slow cooker.76. Smart organizing ideas for your kitchen (Part I).

It's time to get rid of kitchen clutter. You can organize tasks as follows:

    a. Plastic cups and water bottles. Plastic water bottles are not items that you think you might want to keep, right? You should toss them right now. If you have prepared trash bags, it will only take 10 to 15 minutes.

    b. Declutter plastic grocery bags. Bring them together. You can organize a few plastic bags and put them into a tissue box. For the rest of the bags, put them into a large-sized bag and please recycle them. It's so easy to recycle plastic bags!

77. Smart organizing ideas for your kitchen (Part II).

It is time to organize lunch boxes. It will be a 15-minute mission. How to get rid of excess food storage containers? It is easier than you think. But a huge pile of these food containers will fall out each time you open your cupboard. It is even worse when your drawer can not be closed well because it is so stuffed with items. Therefore, you need to get control over these items.

Keep a reasonable amount of lunch boxes. And you should toss or recycle the rest. This is especially true for old margarine and yogurt plastic containers. Margarine and yogurt plastic containers are cheap solutions, but after a long time, they look bad and smell bad, too. Then, you should get rid of all the boxes that no longer had their lids. Afterwards, try to recycle old plastic lunch boxes and the other food storage containers.

78. Smart organizing ideas for your kitchen (Part III).

Serving trays, bowls, platters, utensils and the other party serving pieces take up too much space, but they are rarely used. Only a few times a year. However, they are scattered everywhere in your pantry, in cabinets and drawers. How to keep the beast at bay?

a. Keep the best serving pieces. Nest the items by size on an assigned shelf. Remember –they do not have to stand on your fingertips because you do not use them so often.

b. Throw out damaged serving pieces.

c. Here is a very good tip: square pieces take up less space than round ones! Consider this for the next time when you go shopping.

79. Organize cleaning zone.

Learn to love the uncluttered and clean look of your kitchen. It's time to declutter and organize kitchen cleaning supplies. There are a lot of items, such as all-purpose surface cleaner, sponges, microfiber cloths, scrub brushes, dishwashing liquid, dish gloves, dishwasher detergent, paper towels, trash bags, etc. Things related to cleaning should be organized around the dishwasher and kitchen sink. Organize them in special containers and you will not waste time looking for things. Never again. Make it shine!

80. Kitchen organizing tips: sink front tray.

You know that your sink needs to stay empty and clear most of the time. We have everyday activities in this area of the kitchen, such as washing dishes, cooking, food preparation, etc.

This is an important area because you wash and dry your dishes here. This is the area for storing rags, sponges, dishwashing cloves and the other things. You can install a sink tray in order to hold all clutter that often gathers around a kitchen sink. This isn't so difficult as it seems. Actually, you can buy building products at your local hardware store for $20 - $100 and you will tackle this task over the weekend.

81. Organize under the sink

It's time to clear the clutter around your sink. Catch clutter and reorganize your cleaning area!

a. Take everything out of the cabinet and get rid of anything you never use. It would be great if you are able to discard anything toxic.

b. Clean up this area really well.

c. Now get organized! Purchase new organizers or reuse old organizers. Divide your items among the bins and baskets. Sort by category.

d. You can put dishwasher pods into a sealed tub. You can keep your dish rack under the sink.

82. Labels are great help for keeping kitchen items organized.

There are many computer programs to print your labels. Labels come in printable PDF templates, which are editable. It means that you will be able to change colors, size, font types, etc. Just use different colors for different groups. Then, you have to glue them to containers. From now on, you will always know where everything is. Find these useful templates on the Internet and let your imagination go wild!

83. Keep your veggies organized.

This is a handy tip that can save your space in the pantry. Every family buys a huge amount of vegetables, right? Of course, every family likes salads, stews, soups and the other vegetable dishes. If you are a vegetarian or vegan, the situation is hilarious!

We just leave all our vegetables rolling around on our dining table or kitchen worktops. Sounds familiar?

Therefore, it's time to get your veggies organized! Corral them in a drawer. Place veggies in the wicker baskets. Then, put your baskets into the drawer. You can organize two, three or more drawers, it all depends on the amount of veggies and your personal preferences. Good luck!

84. Organize kitchen cabinets with tension rods.

Do you want to store your favorite pans, tins, cake pans, cookie sheets, and trays near the oven or stove for easy access? Realistically, each of us has a favorite frying pan that we use most frequently. Then, we can have many baking pans but we are constantly preparing cookies in two favorite ones.

You can organize your favorites in a simple way. Install tension curtain rods spaced between shelves in kitchen cabinet. In this way, you can store flat cookware and bakeware and prevent them from piling up. In this manner, you can separate cookware from bakeware and everything will be at your fingertips.

85. Pegboard for small kitchen tools.

You can add a pegboard to your kitchen in order to maximize a vertical space. And you will have a quick and easy access to the frequently used kitchen tools.

a. Purchase the pegboard of choice. Then, paint it in your favorite color.

b. Next, install your pegboard.

Installing a pegboard is a quick and inexpensive way to improve your space. You can also use a metal caddy for this purpose.

86. Get a lot of extra storage with hanging shelves.

There are a lot of kitchen tools that you use on a daily basis. Especially if you love cooking every day. Tired of seeing the clutter in your kitchen? So what to do with these piles of bowls, dishes, spoons, and other kitchen equipment? Dish cloths and towels that are scattered everywhere.

What about hanging shelves? Hanging shelves are inexpensive and practical solutions for small kitchens and tight storage spaces. They are easy to install and you can find them in popular colors and different sizes. The possibilities are endless. Therefore, consider putting hanging shelves into your organization scheme for the kitchen and pantry.

87. You should keep your dishes near the sink.

Store everyday dishes in cabinets near the dishwasher and sink. Toss everything you no longer use. Get rid of chipped plates and other damaged dishes. You can also use wire racks to create multi-level shelving. And you will get an extra storage. It may free up your space. Is anything better than entering into your kitchen and seeing a clean and organized space? Happiness indeed!

88. Two commandments of a clutter-free pantry.

Do you have a system to keep snack packs easily accessible for your children? The solution is setting up a drawer in your pantry to corral snack packs and treats.

a. You can add drawers at the bottom of your pantry. This idea provides quick access to snack foods. Your kids will love this idea. Store these items in the labeled drawer, so that children will always have easy access to them when they come back from school. But remember, be sure to buy healthy treats such as packs of nuts, whole grain cereal, granola bars. That drawer should be low enough for small hands to reach.

b. Secondly, you can store your favorite snacks corralled in clear plastic containers so that your kids can see at a glance what is kept inside. This is a great solution for an afternoon pick-me-up. And you will have less mess, which means – less stress!

89. Let go of sentimental clutter!

If you still have not cleaned the kitchen, it doesn't matter. Here's a life hack for you – it's all good! Of course, you know that clear kitchen is better than cluttered, and yet, it is difficult to begin. You don't like the way your kitchen looks and it holds a spiritual aspect. Somewise. However, you are tired of seeing the clutter in your kitchen. If you are saying now, "Yes, it's my story", don't worry, you are not alone. Millions of people have to deal with this problem.

As always, the simplest solutions are the best. It is very important to have the right attitude. Resolve sentiment and throw away all these unwanted and useless things. You will need garbage bags. Declutter every single drawer and cupboard, no exceptions. Ask yourself: "When have I last used this… pan, pot, knife, etc.?" Let go of sentimental clutter!

Fill your sink with soapy water for a clean-up of dirty items. And so forth. Baby steps.

And remember, work without any pressure. If you got tired, you can finish your job tomorrow. And that's fine. All is well when we move forward!

90. Hang wrapping paper rolls on your closet ceiling.

Do you like to have a few rolls of gift wrap for Holidays? If you always store a couple of gift wrap rolls on hand, this solution will work for you. If you don't have a handy storage, you should consider putting anchor screws in a wall and running galvanized wire in a closet ceiling. And Voila! It will utilize wasted space and colorful rolls of wrapping paper will have their designated spot.

91. Keep drawers organized.

Utilize your drawers to organize heavy-use items that are most frequently used. For example, keep all your peelers together, or all of your rubber scrapers or can openers. If you are lacking empty drawers, adhesive hooks are also great for this purpose. Carefully organize all of your cutting tools such as knives, cheese cutters, scissors, apple slicer, and so on. Afterwards, keep all less common items together. These are items for special occasions like temperature gadgets, pastry tools, or fishing fillet equipment. It's a great look!

92. Designate a drinking zone.

Organize a mini coffee shop in your very own kitchen! You only need to find a spot, e.g. on your countertop to start organizing your favorite drinks. Get rid of your old and useless coffee machine.

a. Choose your favorite coffee machine and you will make this space special. You can purchase a coffee urn, teapot, traditional coffee maker, or espresso machine. It's up to you.

b. Next, keep your most-used cups and mugs handy. You can arrange them on a nice tray. Then, keep your favorite tea and coffee jars well organized in your drink area.

c. After that, organize condiments. Find some pretty vessels to keep your honey, sugar or cream.

d. Afterwards, add wooden disposable stir sticks or washable spoons. Enjoy your coffee!

93. Create your very own cocktail bar.

If you love making cocktails and you already have a few mixers, glasses, and spirits scattered all over your kitchen, it's time to organize them. And make the homemade cocktail bar. Exciting!

A few essential spirits and liquors and a few mixers will do just fine. You will also need recipe book, shaker, strainer, stirring spoons, ice bucket, measuring cups and muddler. You will also need sugar cubes, cocktail skewers, cutting board, knife and pretty glasses. Designate a spot for your mini bar and jazz up your night with homemade cocktails!

94. Solutions for your tiny kitchen.

Here are a few more ideas for your tiny kitchen.

a. You can hang the baskets with fruit and other items that would otherwise be taking up counter space.

b. The false drawer under a sink can be replaced with a tilt-out drawer front.

c. If you have a pantry-less kitchen, consider buying a dresser with deep drawers. You can paint it and get extra space storage.

95. Keep it user-friendly.

Your kitchen is probably the most challenging area in your house. If you're lacking worktops, here are a few solutions.

a. Consider adding a rolling table or cart.

b. Folding wall table is a great option for adding a work surface.

c. You can also purchase 3-in-1 table seats.

You will free up your cramped space and keep it user-friendly.

96. Keep your mugs neat and tidy.

Cups and coffee mugs are fun to shop for, but after a while, most seem to disappear into the darkness of our cupboards. There is a simple question for you – Do you have much more cups than people in your family who use them?

You could free up a lot of space in your cupboards by getting rid of some of them. How about simple hooks? Hanging mugs from hooks along the bottom of a shelf will free up kitchen space and it also looks cozy.

Then, if you have any extra shelf, it would be great. You can also maximize the storage by using racks on the shelves.

Declutter your kitchen, declutter your life!

97. Store your supplements and vitamins.

Decluttered vitamins can make a mess in every house. Here are a few steps to keep them well organized.

Step one: Bring all vitamins together.

Step two: Check all expiration dates; get rid of expired items.

Step three: Leave vitamins in their original containers. When storing your vitamins, be sure to keep them away from extreme temperatures. The best solution is a cupboard away from the oven. Brilliant!

BATHROOM

Make your bathroom sparkle and shine!

Bathroom needs a systematic plan for organizing and decluttering. Divide your space into three zones and declutter each and every bit of your bathroom. Putting your bathroom items back is as easy as ABC. Afterwards, prepare a relaxing bath and enjoy!

98. Buy organizing products by considering the bigger picture.

First of all, you have to set up certain spots for certain items. What to do further? Of course, you should buy specific organizing products. Or you can make them yourself. Just make sure to buy organizing products that match the décor of your space. For example, you can use plastic containers for your bathroom but you will not use them for your living room with solid wood furniture. You can put some plastic items in kids' room, too. It is important to make a difference and consider the aesthetics. If you have no idea what to purchase and find this difficult, stick to a simple rule – The simpler, the better! Once you've purchased a new organizing product, use it to improve your life. And you will wonder how you ever got along without them!

99. Decluttering missions for the entire bathroom.

Take the 10-10-10 challenge! This would mean:

- 10 items to be repaired and returned to the positions to which they belong;

- 10 items to throw away;

- 10 items to donate;

It will be an exciting way to organize 30 things in your bathroom right now. This challenge is an incredibly fun to take so that children will join you willingly. What's the best of all? This challenge will become an entertaining competition between your kids. Keep this tip in your back pocket and use it every time when your bathroom is a total mess. You can use this trick in any part of your house. The principles remained the same.

100. Let dust be your guide!

Do you have troubles organizing the bathroom's limited space? Do you really need that comb with missing teeth? What about that fraying toothbrush? Realistically, your bathroom is an activity-intensive room. Accessing shower gel, soap, shampoo or conditioner can be annoying when they aren't stored at your fingertips.

First of all, take a black plastic garbage bag and throw away broken items, valueless products, empty bottles, and so on. Even half-used products. If you haven't used that lotion for six months or the past year, you probably never will. Here is a simple trick – dust can be your guide. It means, any product with a dusty coating goes to the trash right now!

Next, use a box that is designated as "donate box" for surplus products that are still useful. The whole process will take less than 15 minutes. Declutter your bathroom once and for all!

101. A systematic plan for your bathroom.

Bathroom needs a systematic plan for storing and organizing . Try to divide your space into three zones.

    a. **The first zone** is designated for everyday items. E.g. soap, toothbrushes, the shampoo, shower gel, and the razor. This zone should be user-friendly and very accessible. Store these items on countertop, in the top drawer, or in hanging baskets.

    b. **The second zone** holds items that are used weekly and monthly. E.g. makeup, perfumes, nail care equipment. Store them in the middle drawer and on the toilet-top storage cupboard, taking care to give the items easily accessible spots.

    c. **The third zone** is designated for the items that are rarely used. It includes under-sink space and the shelf above the bathroom door.

102. Keep your bathroom clutter-free and sparkling!

There are a lot of products that can make your bathroom sparkle. Household cleaning cloths, wipes, mops, cleaning brushes, scouring pad, glass cleaners, microfiber cloths, etc. However, all of these small products could make clutter because they never have their designated place. And you still have a mess in the bathroom.

Your goal is to clean and organize your bathroom in a short time, so you can get on with the more important and funnier things in your life. The solution is easier than you think. Add a tension rod underneath a bathroom cabinet to maximize space. Then, hang "S-hooks" for storing your cleaning products as well as the other bathroom supplies. You can also add a second tension rod for even more space.

103. End your day with a clean bathroom cabinet.

Is there anything better than walking up into a clean space? Get this done today and you will be a happier in the evening. This easy task will affect your mood for the rest of your day for sure. Ready, set, go!

a. First of all, take everything out of the cabinet.

b. Then, wipe down the interior and shelves.

c. Have a trash bag on hand and toss unwanted items. Dispose of everything that you haven't used in the last year and everything that is empty and nearly empty.

d. Create your shopping list.

In this way, you'll be able to simplify the clutter so that you can enjoy your bathroom to the fullest.

104. Cut clutter in the bathroom – Shower and bath caddies.

Personal hygiene products are scattered all over your bathroom. And you hate all that mess! Keeping your bathroom tidy and organized can be challenging. However, with a goodwill you can win this battle.

Your favorite moisturizers, lotions, deodorants and the other products can be cleverly organized and stored. Try hanging a bath caddy! You should hang it on a hook mounted on the wall and the problem is solved. Shower and bath caddies will declutter the floor of your bathroom. Therefore, install this great item close to your bathtub or hang it in your shower cabin, and take a shower right now! You can use bath caddies in order to organize your makeup, too. After decluttering, prepare a relaxing bath and enjoy!

105. Under the bathroom sink.

Are you embarrassed to let anyone come into your bathroom? Is your bathroom sink cabinet is jammed with unwanted items? There is no doubt – clutter can really influence the way you live. Here're simple hacks for decluttering bathroom sink cabinet.

a. Take everything out and lay it on the ground.

b. Throw out or recycle everything that is broken and useless.

c. Wipe down your bathroom sink cabinet.

d. Reorganize your tools by categories. Use baskets to keep them neat and tidy.

Your bathroom will be in order and you will be happy!

106. Under-the-sink storage ideas.

Here are some creative ideas to organize useful space under your sink.

a. Keep your cleaning supplies and tools in an easy-to-grab basket so you can take it every time you start cleaning.

b. Fill another basket with boxes of tissue or extra toilet paper.

c. Hang spray bottles on a tension rod.

d. Place large-sized items such as toilet brush and bottles in the back.

107. Clever and practical: over-the-door bin.

This bin is ideal for a cramped space in a bathroom cabinet. It can hold your hair brushes, favorite styling products, hair dryer and other items. It's a great way to utilize empty space in bathroom cabinets. Never search your home again for your favorite styling tools with this handy over-the-door bin!

108. A simple way to store more in your bathroom.

Tired of wasting time searching for a bath item you need? A shoe holder is a simple but great organizer that can be used in many different ways. The possibilities are endless. Anyway, this is a wonderful way to declutter and organize your bathroom. You can attach a shoe holder to the inside of a bathroom cabinet. And you will get an extra storage for your bottles, cleaners, spray bottles, cosmetic products, and so on.

Catch clutter and reorganize your bathroom! Happiness indeed!

109. Keep your beauty product neat and tidy in a small bathroom.

Small bathroom? No worries, there are so many creative solutions to keep your miniature bathroom well organized.

First of all, you have to declutter your bathroom. Get rid of all unwanted products and tools.

Now you should designate spots for each and every bathroom item. Make a use of every nook in your bathroom by hanging baskets or bags with handles on stylish hooks. It's best to purchase uniform hanging baskets due to the aesthetic effect.

110. Floating shelves – a brilliant idea for small bathroom.

Use floating shelves to create extra storage in your miniature bathroom. They are perfect to stash extra towels and other items. The benefits are obvious. In this way, you will use every inch, and space will be clutter-free at the same time. Floating shelves fit in narrow spaces and they can corral a lot of bathroom essentials.

111. Three storage tricks for a tiny bathroom.

a. Save space by stacking your products in a decorative magazine holder. It is a thin and useful organizer.

b. Hang your hairdryer and hair curlers on adhesive hooks inside of a bathroom cabinet door.

c. Organize your bottles, deodorants, and lotions on an old wine rack and save space in bathroom. You can paint the rack and get a stylish organizer.

These organization tricks will leave you feeling great and refreshed.

112. A quick way to clean your medicine cabinet.

Create one spot for medicines. Bring the medicines into one place. First, get rid of outdated stuff and utilized items such as the dirty bandages, the old creams, expired ointments and drugs, as well as all medicines that did not have any effect on your health problems. Get rid of "just in case" items because these things take up space, and, honestly, they weigh us down. Therefore, free up your space for more beautiful things than drugs and medicaments.

113. A cheap and clever way to store bath toys.

Bathtub toys can create a huge clutter in your bathroom. If they are scattered all over the bathroom and fall down on the floor, it's time for decluttering.

You can simply hang a multilevel fruit basket for additional storage. Take advantage of vertical storage and you will declutter your bathroom instantly. A fruit basket can be used as a caddy so that water drains out, and the toys are easy for your child to reach. This idea works for kid's shampoo, sponges, and other bath accessories. Try to hang the fruit basket in an unused corner. Put bath toys into the basket and you will keep toys in one place. If you have a tiny bathroom, it will save the space a lot. Brilliant!

114. A magnetic strip – organize small metal grooming items.

Nail clippers, tweezers, bobby pins, hairpins and other small metal items are scattered everywhere in your bathroom. Tired of searching for your small metal grooming aids?

Install a magnet to hold all these super useful metal items! You can add a magnetic strip to the inside of a medicine cabinet or other storage area. It's up to you!

a. You can buy a magnetic tape at any home improvement store.

b. Then, you should cut a magnetic strip in order to fit your medicine cabinet; peel away the cover on the tape side.

c. Arrange your small metal items. You can do it yourself!

115. A clever solution for toilet paper.

If you purchase bulk paper towels, you probably have a problem to store them. How about shoe bags? Put the bags into bathroom closet and that's it. In this way, you'll be able to simplify the clutter in your bathroom so that you can enjoy this space to the fullest. Clever.

116. Organize a complete makeup (Part I).

Are you a makeup addict? Do you spend money buying duplicates for beauty products and tools you already have? Are your products are scattered all over the bathroom? Even a small amount of beauty products can make your bathroom look cluttered. If you feel helpless because you can't solve the problem, you are not alone. There is a solution. Follow these few steps and you will declutter your makeup products easily and effortlessly.

Ready, set, go!

a. It's time to start throwing out the unwanted products. Gather up all of your beauty products. Check expiration dates.

b. Try your best to minimize the number of beauty products in your home. If you can't remember the last time you used a beauty product, ask yourself, "Can I see myself using this again?"

c. Clean up your beauty products. It would be good if you use a mat for powdery mess.

d. After that, you should find a convenient place to store your favorite products.

And from now on, when you want to find some beauty product, you'll always know where it is. The clutter-cutting benefits are obvious! Lovely!

117. Organize a complete makeup (Part II).

You buy all kinds of makeup products because they make you look and feel better, right? Do you keep your makeup and beauty products well organized? If your makeup is a mess, you can't enjoy it to the fullest. There is no doubt, one of the best solution to keep your makeup organized is a drawer with dividers. Group makeup products in a way that is logical to you. Toss unwanted makeup. Determine how to best organize what's left by grouping your beauty products by type and frequency of use. Enjoy doing your makeup!

118. An ingenious idea for storing your small beauty products.

Are your makeup products like eye shadow, mascara, and lipstick are scattered all over the bathroom cabinet?

Put your everyday small beauty products into an easily accessible spot. Consider using a jewelry organizer to visibly store all these small items. If you're lacking cabinet space, this will be a great idea for you! And from now on, when you want to find your favorite mascara or lipstick, you'll always know where it is.

119. A cookie jar and a cupcake tray in your bathroom.

Out of sight means less visual clutter, but things hidden in the bathroom cabinet tend to be forgotten.

Here are two amazing and chip hacks for decluttering and organizing bathroom accessories, makeup, etc. Make them visible and easily accessible. You can use a cookie jar to store your lip glosses or nail polishes. Then, you can stack your makeup products on the tiers of a cupcake tray. In this way, you can group them by categories.

120. Change your habits – change your bathroom.

Duplicates. This clutter is demanding of you a lot of hard-earned money. Group items in a way that is logical to you. Designate a spot for all your duplicates and extras. A plastic container works well. When you run out of any product, check that container to see if you already have it on hand.

121. Personalized bathroom shelves.

If you have space on the wall, consider installing personalized boxes. You will have a cute storage box for each family member. You can store items your family use most frequently so they should be easily reachable. You can paint these shelves so each family member will have her/his favorite color. Cute!

122. Organize your nail polishes.

You love nail polishes, there are dozens of them. They are scattered all over the house. And you know why? Because they don't have their designated spot. If you have an old spice rack, you will find an ideal home for your nail polishes. You can also store essential oils there. You may paint this spice rack using a color of choice.

123. Two cheap solutions to keep your perfume collection organized.

You can organize overflowing bathroom with these unusual life hacks. First of all, gather up all perfume bottles. Now get rid of empty bottles and unwanted perfumes. Use these cheap organizers:

a. A spice rack can be a perfect shelf for your fragrances.

b. You can also display your perfume bottles on top of a cake stand.

124. How to organize your drawers once and for all?

Bathroom drawers can work wonders to tame clutter. We often wonder how bathroom drawers get so messy?

a. First, take the drawers out and empty them. Bring all items together. Check expiration dates and check each and every item. Ask yourself, "Can I see myself using this again". If you think you will never use it again, simply throw it away.

b. Clean up your drawers.

c. Then, you can decorate your drawers. You can coat the inside of your drawers with wallpaper cut to fit.

Use drawer dividers and decluttering-smart clear bins to take the organization to the next level!

125. Solve overstuffed drawers.

With the right setup, there's a place for each and every bathroom item.

After decluttering, create three piles:

1) Items that should go in the drawer;

2) Stuff that shouldn't go in the drawer;

3) Clutter and garbage.

Deal with the clutter immediately and group necessary items by category. For example, tuck your hairdryer and other corded appliances in a basket; then, put the basket into decluttered drawer. Put the rest of your items back in place using the baskets. As you can see, the solution is simpler than you thought.

126. Use utensil tray for your favorite beauty products.

Are your tweezers, lipsticks, mascara, makeup brushes, and the other beauty products scattered in your bathroom? Place the utensil tray in a drawer in the bathroom to keep these items organized. This is really useful for all these small items that every girl has in her life. Create your beauty zone without any investment. Lovely!

127. Organize your hair accessories.

You are doing your hair and you need some bobby pins urgently. Where are the thousands of bobby pins you bought? Hair clips, hair grips, barrettes, hair bands… there are too much items. This is a budget-friendly way to organize your favorite cheap but valuable small items. Actually, you will need zero dollars!

You can clean an old shoe box and use it for all your hair trinkets. Cover the box with wrapping paper of choice. And Voila! Bask in the glory of your new lifestyle!

128. A fun way to organize trinkets.

Girls love trinkets. Earrings, bracelets, necklace, etc. Yours or your daughter's costume jewelry deserves a special "home". However, it does not have to be an expensive box or jewelry holder. You can use mason jars! You can also add some labels to group your jewelry. Then, you can paint your jars, wrap a fancy ribbon around them, add lace and tinsels. You will have great and inexpensive jewelry storage. At the same time, you will have fun decorating your jars.

129. Hair ties, ponytail holders, and headbands.

For everyday hairstyle, make sure you're stocked up on essential hair accessories. Nevertheless, they are scattered throughout the bathroom, bedroom, and the other rooms. And they create clutter! Realistically, how many of those trinkets do you need? Therefore, get rid of old and useless headbands and ties. Free yourself from this type of clutter.

You can use an oatmeal container for hair accessories storage. Or you can purchase an inexpensive decorative bin for that purpose.

130. A solution for storing spray bottles.

Do you have a great amount of spray bottles in your bathroom? Various types of bathroom cleaners, disinfecting spray cleaners, floor cleaners, glass cleaner, and so on. You are aware that you have to free up all that space in your bathroom. How to do it?

The tension rod is a simple and effective solution! Install tension rod in a bathroom closet. You even don't have to pay a handyman; it's not rocket science. You can do it yourself and free up space in your bathroom significantly. Putting the spray bottles back is as easy as ABC. Give it a try!

131. Items that are rarely used.

When it comes to organizing the bathroom, there are some items that are rarely used. For instance, guest towels or holiday party curling iron. Yes, it's true, they are rarely used but they are necessary from time to time. And they can make a lot of clutter. A shelf above the bathroom door is a great spot for these items. Well-organized bathroom truly makes our lives easier.

DINING ROOM

The importance of eating together

Is your dining room a catch-all for clutter? It's time to win your battle with clutter. There's nothing more beautiful than waking up to a clean dining room space.

Dining room promotes healthy eating at home so keep it neat and tidy. Get your dining room shipshape!

132. The "three-box" method for your dining room.

First, you should buy three boxes. They will be: "keep", "give away", and "trash".

As you set out to declutter your dining room, this interesting technique will help you a lot. This also can be super funny competition between you and your kids or you and your husband.

Each and every item in your dining room should be placed into one of the three categories. All without exception. Remember – no item was passed over!

133. Declutter dining room cabinet.

You should find space for your porcelain dinnerware sets, tablecloths, candles, expensive glasses, napkins and other items. Dining storage allows you to keep everything neat and tidy. However, if your dining storage is jammed with clutter, you probably waste your time searching for a certain item. Luckily, there is a great way to declutter dining room cabinets.

   a. **Step one:** Take everything out including cabinet organizers like shelf dividers. It will help you to see the available space in the cabinet.

   b. **Step two:** Wipe down your cabinet and remove dust and spills.

   c. **Step three:** This is the fun part. You should make six piles – "keep in cabinet", "put away in another place", "give away", "sell", "trash", and "recycle (repurpose)".

Keep in mind – Small appliances are fun to shop for, but after a while, most of them seem to disappear into the darkness of your cabinet. Some of them have sentimental significance, but you don't use them and they just gather dust. Resolve sentiment and throw away all these unwanted and useless things.

Now, you are ready to organize your dining room cabinet.

134. Keep dining room cabinet organized.

Is your dining room a catch-all for clutter? Most of the odds end up in the corner of your cabinet. This plan will get your cabinet in shape and help prevent clutter from building up in the future.

First, you should find a place for things you use every day. They should be at your fingertips. If you have limited space in your cabinet, remove rarely used items to the another place in the house. In this way, you can easily organize your casual dinnerware and everyday items such as a tablecloth, napkins, cutlery, etc.

Sort by category: for example, 1) napkins and napkin rings, 2) cutlery, etc.

Now, you only need to maintain this new clutter-free environment you've created. Bravo!

135. How to maintain a decluttered dining room?

Yes, the clutter defines a part of you as a person. For example, if you love magazines or books, these things reflect your passion and this is quite normal. If you enjoy browsing through magazines in your dining room, this is quite normal, too. But you should be organized. Do not leave magazines scattered on the dining table. How to maintain decluttered dining room?

a. Try to spend ten minutes each evening clearing out everything that doesn't belong in your dining room.

b. Then, each time you plan to buy something new for your dining room, search through your drawers and cabinets so you do not buy duplicates.

c. It is important to sort through your dining room cabinets at the start of each season.

136. Declutter the dining room table.

Any type of clutter tends to accumulate on your dining room table if kitchen accessories and other items don't have a designated place where they are stored. So take the time to declutter and clear off your table.

a. **Step one:** Bring them all together and start sorting into three categories: "kitchen accessories", "other accessories", and "dining room accessories". It will take less than 10 minutes.

b. **Step two:** Now you need to find a spot for each and every item. Put away things that do not belong here. Things that belong in the kitchen, take them to the kitchen. The other things will need their "homes" in the other rooms of the house.

c. **Step three:** arrange items from the third category and keep them organized on your dining table.

Afterwards, to maintain a clear dining table henceforward, you will need to find homes for all the things that seem to accumulate on your dining table. That's all you've got to do.

137. Promote beauty and order.

Retake the valuable surface of your dining table with this simple hack. This trick works for the most of the people. Put something pretty, such as flower arrangement, on the dining table. You will discourage placing all sorts of things on your table. Easy.

138. Corral kids' belongings.

If your children use the dining table for board games and homework, no big deal.   However, that's not the main purpose of the kitchen table. Teach them to clear the supplies off dining table after each usage. Then, they should store their belongings at the place designated. It is very important for small items such as toy bricks and blocks, pencils and the other school supplies. These items can create clutter and you should control it. Nevertheless, the best solution is to set up desks or work table for those activities.

139. Dining room organizations – baskets.

If you find you can't use your dining room for what it meant to do because of certain reasons, it's time to solve this problem. There are a lot of reasons you should use your dining room more frequently. The family dining room is more than a place to eat. This is the area where the family can sit down together and socialize with one another. The dining room is perfect for gatherings with family and friends. However, if your dining room is jammed with stuff, it cannot serve its purpose.

Baskets are perfect organization tools for this kind of room. You can keep a lot of things in them. In that way, you will remove clutter from table, chairs and display cabinets. If your dining room is filled with knick-knacks, candles, lighters, napkins, and other small items, consider buying pretty straw baskets. You can go one step further and purchase the baskets with handles to hang them on a wall with hooks.

140. Use dresser in your dining room.

Dresser is the super organizing piece of furniture. You can find an old dresser or even an antique dresser at garage sales.

Now you can keep silverware, china, linens, candles, hand wipes and other things well organized. You can divide and organize items by categories or frequency of use. For example, designate drawers for the following categories:

- napkins,

- tablecloths,

- disposable dishes,

- place mats, etc.

141. Keep your sideboard neat and tidy.

Coasters, china, stemware, silverware bottle openers, and so on. There are a lot of things in your sideboard. This piece of furniture is designed to hold so many items and because of that it is perfect for your dining room. How to keep it organized and enjoy your dining room to the fullest?

a. Set aside some time, e.g. on Saturday morning, after family breakfast. Remove everything from the sideboard and bring together. Toss damaged, broken, and useless things. Donate duplicates and things that you will never use again.

b. Further, wipe down your sideboard and remove dust and spills. Clean and polish each item.

c. Create groups for all things that you will put back on the sideboard. Designate a spot for each group of items. Decide how to store them: vertically or horizontally. Arrange your items and enjoy the new look of your sideboard!

142. Your cocktail cabinet.

Do you like cocktails and romantic dinners? Are your spirits and liquors scattered all over kitchen and dining room? If your answer is yes – consider organizing a cocktail cabinet.

a. Sort items into categories.

b. Assign a space for your mixers, ice buckets shakers, trays, and other cocktail party equipment.

c. Assign a space for the bottles and group them into categories.

d. Line the shelves with paper or cork linings and place your glasses on it. Keep glasses upright and in widely spaced rows.

143. Extra storage – rolling bar cart.

Wheeled furniture is always a great solution. This is the especially good idea for small space. If you need an extra counter space, consider buying a cart. You can organize everything in a simple and practical way.

You can also transport your dishes from kitchen to dining room using this cart. You can find a metal cart with glass and bottle support. A small rolling bar cart is just what you need to make things more manageable. And you can place your cart anywhere you want.

144. You get a lot of extra storage with hanging shelves.

There are a lot of things that we use on a daily basis. We just need these items each and every day. Especially if we have kids. Parents are aware of it. However, what to do with this pile of toys, newspapers, books, groceries and other items that are scattered all over dining room? When it comes to clearing clutter from your dining room, these things are the first in the list.

Are you looking for a daily activity organizer? What about floating shelves? Floating shelves are inexpensive and practical solutions for your dining room. They are easy to install and you can find them in popular colors and different sizes depending on their purpose. The possibilities are endless.

145. Sort your newspapers and magazines.

You love your magazines so much. However, do you have magazine holders? Or do you have a special home for them, for example, on a bookshelf? If your answer is No, it's time to sort your favorite magazines. Here are a few steps to do that easily and effortlessly.

    a.   Decide which magazines you need to keep. If your answer is – "I probably should read", get them out of your house.

b. If you need to read some magazines for work assignment or your kids need some of them for school, you can keep them.

c. Therefore, you should organize them and put them into the place designated. A good solution is to purchase a couple of magazine racks.

146. Wheeled furniture for small living space.

This is a life hack that can help you to declutter fast and easy.

Wheeled tables, desks, and wastebaskets offer the advantage of being easily moved. You can find even ottomans, side tables, and chairs on wheels. They are perfect for a cramped space because they can easily be repositioned.

147. How to throw a dinner party in a small apartment?

You have a small dining room or you don't have that space at all, but you love parties. Don't let a small space hold you back! Here are some tricks to make it a snap.

a. A living room with the furniture moved out of the way can make a great space for your dinner party.

b. Use folding chairs that can be easily replaced. Your guests can sit on pillows, why not?!

c. If you can't make a dining table works in your living, throw a cocktail party with appetizers. To serve, use large platters on a coffee table as well as carts and wheeled furniture.

148. Weeknight dinner party – keep party supplies on hand.

It's time to declutter your party supplies. Toss everything that is broken and useless. You can use a large-sized shoe box and label it "Party Box". Keep the necessities in this box.

Your party box will include balloons, candles, streamers, etc. And you'll have peace of mind knowing that you're well prepared.

Then, choose your favorite party recipes and enjoy the fun. There is a money saving hack: remember to shop sales after the holidays. Prices for party supplies are the lowest at this time.

BEDROOM

Get your bedroom in tip-top shape!

"Three Rules of Work: Out of clutter find simplicity; From discord find harmony; In the middle of difficulty lies opportunity." – Albert Einstein

Get rid of unwanted items and opt for small pieces of furniture. You will free up your space significantly! It might seem like a daunting task, but you can start with baby steps. Declutter one area at a time and don't move to the next zone until you have finished the previous.

It is such a relief and happiness to have all those items finally sorted! Get your bedroom in tip-top shape!

149. Get organized – divide into zones.

As you probably know, it's easy to let a room turn chaotic. Use these simple rules to streamline your bedroom. Actually, one of the best methods to tackle the problem is to divide your bedroom into areas. There are three main zones: 1) the sleeping zone; 2) the relaxing and entertaining zone; 3) the grooming zone. There are many of us that have the fourth part and it is the work zone.

Everything in your bedroom should fit into one of these three or four categories. If you have an item that doesn't fit, it may not belong in your bedroom.

Declutter one area at a time and don't move to the next zone until you have finished the previous. Good luck!

150. Declutter your bedroom – surplus furniture.

Is your bedroom jammed with furniture? Having too many chairs, tables, dressers, and other things makes the bedroom appear smaller.

a. Get rid of surplus furniture and you'll get more space for you. Think about what you can sell or donate. You can sell them at garage sale or you can give them away. You should use only the pieces that are necessary for your bedroom to function. Remember – less is more!

b. Clean your room thoroughly.

c. The way you arrange furniture can make a big difference. Find a spot for each and every piece that makes the most sense to you.

d. Add a new decoration, maybe a picture. Enjoy your new bedroom.

151. Handy tips to help declutter your bedroom.

"Three Rules of Work: Out of clutter find simplicity; From discord find harmony; In the middle of difficulty lies opportunity." – Albert Einstein

a. **Step one:** While you are going through this mess, ask yourself: Do I really need all these things in my bedroom? Is anything in this area unused? Toss unwanted items.

b. **Step two:** This is the fun part. You should make six piles – keep, put away in another place, give away, sell, trash, and recycle (repurpose). If there are items that could be useful to someone, give it to them.

c. **Step three:** Designate a spot for each and every item. Put items back in their places.

To maintain this decluttered environment, stick to a few important rules:

a. Make your bed every morning.

b. Keep your clothes organized. Place them in your closet or in the laundry basket.

c. Avoid bedside clutter.

d. Do not ruin what you have achieved.

152. Turn a dresser into bedside tables.

There are a lot of random items under your bed, on the floor and all over the bedroom. You can replace your side tables for dressers and get some extra storage for all your small items and tchotchkes. Of course, this trick will not spoil the aesthetics of the room.

153. Use the advantage of hidden storage.

If you are looking for a place to keep your sports equipment, blankets, nighttime necessities and other things, wicker trunk is a perfect solution. This cute hidden storage has plenty of space and it also gives the bedroom an elegant decorative effect and evokes a homey feel.

154. Turn bedroom clutter into décor.

If lots of items are littering your floor, you can arrange them in an artful way. You can stack your big fat books and get a nice decor. You can arrange magazines in the same fashion. This is a little change, but it can apparently transform your bedroom. It is such a relief and happiness to have them finally sorted!

155. Rolling cart for your bedroom.

If you wonder how to live a more organized life, here's a simple hack. Use a rolling chart in your bedroom!

This amazing chart can be used as a bedside table. Consider buying the cart with a drawer so you can keep jewelry, keys, and other favorites well organized. This cart can also hide everyday clutter. The possibilities are endless, so be creative!

156. Small furniture will open up your space.

No matter how big your bedroom is, opt for small pieces of furniture and you will free up your space significantly. It's better to have a few pieces with drawers and a few floating shelves than a large closet. In this way, you will achieve the better results because each and every item will find their "home". In the large closet, they could be scattered and invisible.

157. Get organized: use dividers.

All these small items create a lot of clutter in your bedroom. It might seem like a daunting task, but you can start with baby steps. Luckily, there are drawer dividers to keep all items neat and tidy. You can also use small dishes such as vintage cups. Don't throw your accessories into a large drawer once you get home. Divide the drawers and put every item back into a designated spot. Get your bedroom in tip-top shape!

158. Hang instead of stand.

You can hang a wicker basket to save space in your bedroom. You can use this basket for your socks, slippers, scarves, mittens, etc. This is a perfect spot for items that we usually throw somewhere in the bedroom once we get home

159. Organization hacks for your tiny bedroom.

You have a tiny bedroom. Fortunately, there are a lot of great tricks to make the most of your room.

Consider buying a console table. It will be used as a shelf and a desk. This is a great place for your morning coffee, magazines, a book, glasses, etc. And you will feel good. Feeling good can be a way of life.

160. Maximizing under-bed storage.

It is a great place to keep an alarm clock, your magazines, books, reading glasses, tissues, and so on. You will have more useful space in your bedroom. And of course, some things will be hidden so they do not spoil the aesthetics of the room. Great!

161. Turn your desk into a bedside table.

You do not have to have a large bedroom in order to be happy. Balance is the key to a happy bedroom. Don't overfill your space with a lot of things. Here's a hack that will save a lot of space. Simply place your desk next to the bed and you will get two in one!

162. Declutter your bedroom and sleep peacefully.

Within the walls of our home, we try to live a balanced life. The key to a balanced life is organization. Bedroom allows us to express our creativity through organizing and decorating. In terms of creativity, do you really need a footboard? If you have a tiny bedroom, it can be a completely unnecessary piece of furniture. Therefore, put your desk instead of the footboard. Great idea!

Remember – Take control of your clutter! Everyone can designate five minutes a day to put things away. Remove anything that doesn't belong in the bedroom and go to sleep.163. Use every corner in your tiny bedroom.

If you don't have a closet in the bedroom, you can hang your clothes on a tension rod. You can also hang towels and other items. If you are a fan of the simplicity, this is a right solution for you. And when you want to find some item, you will always know where it is.

164. Declutter and organize your relaxing zone.

Is your relaxing zone jammed with items, so you are not able to relax there? Organization of relaxing zone requires decluttering, cleaning, and sorting to make your space a calming haven. You can tackle this problem with a few simple hacks!

a. Gather decluttering tools such as garbage boxes and bags. Bring all items together and sort all items. Create six piles: keep, put away in another place, give away, sell, trash, and recycle (repurpose). Sort each item into one of the piles. Work systematically around the entire space.

b. Toss unwanted items.

c. Take a duster and clean your ornaments, lamps, vases and other items such as guitars, painting equipment, books, etc.

d. Get it tidy! Put everything back and enjoy the new look of your bedroom. To soften this area, organize your pillows.

There's nothing more beautiful than waking up to a clean space.

165. Dealing with clutter according to your personality – Sentimentalist.

"If you know the enemy and know yourself you need not fear the results of a hundred battles." – Sun Tzu

You can stop clutter session in the bedroom once and for all if you know yourself! As you declutter and organize, pay attention to the root of the problem. Your bedroom reveals more about you. If you are a sentimentalist, you probably have a box of unsorted photos in the corner of your bedroom. Or you have the Teddy Bear collection from your childhood.

Learn to let go. However, take your time. It's not going to get better by pushing yourself too hard. Work in short intervals, take a break, and enjoy a cup of tea or lunch.

Free your mind. Go for a short walk or take a shower. Do meditation and calm your mind. A fresh mind will help you make smarter decisions.

Self-examination. Take a random item and ask yourself: What's significant about this item? Do I like it enough to display it further? Can I give someone else my stuff? Of course, you do not have to get rid of everything. Save the best items and get rid of the rest.

Enlist help if you need it. Remember – you are not alone. And little by little, it will set you free!

166. Under bed boxes and storage to save your space.

Sometimes you do not know where to put large items such as coats, blankets, bed sets and similar things. There is a lot of space under your bad, right? The whole box with blankets, duvet covers, pillows, and bedding sets could fit there.

Once you use these items, you will be surprised by its benefits. You can keep things like winter clothes in this under bed storage boxes. Therefore, these items stay out of your way but they're still close at hand. Give it a try and keep your room in tip-top shape!

167. Declutter the work zone.

It is the time to organize place where you do homework, study or work. Here are some guidelines:

a. Gather decluttering tools such as garbage bags. Bring all items together. You should have four garbage bags: keep, give away, sell, and trash. Sort each item into one of the piles.

b. Then, throw unwanted items away. Toss everything that is broken, rusty, useless, etc.

c. It's not enough for your workspace to be tidy — it must be clean, too. Take a duster and clean your stuff.

d. Put everything back and enjoy your new desk.

Remember – you can turn your workspace into a clutter-free paradise!

168. Change your habits, change your workspace for the better.

Your penholder contains a lot of pencils, but only one pen works. And many of your pencils are dry. Then, you have a lot of junk mail on your desk. Your penholder is old and dusty. So you need to start throwing the old paper, boxes, pencils, and so on. Otherwise there will be no space for you in this room. Clutter makes you confused and distracted. The scientists believe that a huge number of things that make you happy are within your control.

So, help yourself in an easy way. Close your eyes, breathe deeply and visualize neat and tidy workspace. Enjoy your visualization for a few minutes. Focus on the result – productivity without stress and confusion. Feel happiness and calmness. It will increase your chances to declutter your desk right now. By practicing this mental exercise for 5 to 6 minutes a day, you will be happy to put your desk in order at the end of each working day. Make a list of your obligations for the next day and you will form a new good habit. Good luck!

169. One of the best organizers of all time – command hooks.

Attach hooks on the wall next to the desk and you'll get extra storage space for your workspace. Hang your backpacks, laptop bag, purse, and the other bags that you need for work. Be inspired by command hooks!

There are lots of ways to use command hooks. Here're some of them:

a. You can use two hooks to make wrapping paper easy to tear. It can be a great solution for adhesive tapes, too.

b. Then, hang a wire file box on the side of your desk.

c. You can use special hooks for holding cords.

d. You can design a paper towel holder with two hooks and a spare wire.

170. Baskets for your work zone.

Here's a great hack for your work zone, especially for those with tiny workspace – Use hooks to hang baskets on the wall! You can use old wire basket and paint them to add vintage charm to your space.

This trick makes your everyday job beautiful! Of course, this system will be easy to maintain because your items are in sight. You will be so happy that your tiny workspace has clean surfaces and a bit of personality.

171. Desk makeover – never enough baskets.

Position buckets on the side of your craft table or work desk and you'll get extra space storage for your small items. Add baskets to hold your necessities and trinkets. You will have all these items at your fingertips and desk will be clutter-free! And remember – it must be inspiring!

172. Think outside the shelf.

Turn your wire storage baskets on their sides, attach them to the wall, and you've got stunning shelves! Turn boring wire baskets into functional storage solution. These unconventional shelves are both fun and practical. You can also use nesting basket and get wall-mounted baskets for your room. Adorable!

173. Use empty cans to create your desk organizer.

There is no doubt – clutter can really influence the way you think and work. If you are looking for an easy way to organize your home office here's a simple hack for decluttering your workspace.

You can use empty cans for pencils, markers, rulers, scissors, adhesive tapes and the other useful items. All you have to do is to clean up a few tin cans and cover them with a trendy color of your choice. And you get the clever desk organizer!

174. A high-level organization – rolling cart.

If you have lots of small items at your workstation a rolling cart is the right solution. There is another huge advantage – this cart is small enough to fit under your desk.

You can place it in a corner, too. And you will be able to transfer it wherever you want. Lovely!

175. Maximize storage space in your workstation.

This is an inexpensive and simple solution for cluttered workspace. You will use wall space and free up the rest of the workspace. Consider installing freestanding wall units and declutter your workstation.

176. Handle paperwork, documents and mail.

"You can't have everything. Where would you put it?" – Steven Wright

Does your workplace look like this: you have piles and piles of papers on your desk? There are lots of papers scattered on your desk. And you have no system to organize them. Not at all.

The person who works in a messy workspace spends a lot of time looking for things. This person can be also distracted by unnecessary things. Here is a trick to free up your workspace and increase your work capacity.

In terms of papers and documents, ask yourself: Is this item essential? It is really important question, especially if you tend to save material "just in case". Bring your papers all together. You can extract the information from these materials and store it in a minimized form. Therefore, go digital – switch to paperless statements and scan as much as you can. You should digitalize your business as much as you can and eliminate paper clutter forever.

177. Create a spot for incoming papers.

You used to have piles and piles of incoming papers. Various notices, receipts, manuals, flyers, warranties and the other papers. The whole family, including you, put them into different spots and they are scattered all over the house – on the kitchen table, on the dresser in the hallway, on the counter, etc. Even all over your car. So you can't find anything! Stop battling with the paper clutter once and for all!

Designate an in-box tray in a certain location of your home. Put each and every paper into that in-box tray. Got some papers? Put it into your inbox. Done! This is a little change, but it can apparently transform your paperwork. It is such a relief and happiness to have them finally sorted!

178. You can easily sort the files.

A mountain of paperwork is a nightmare for many people. The reason is simple. We didn't create a good spot for them and papers keep piling up for days, weeks, months... No worries, the solution is at your fingertips. You can organize some simple folders.

First of all, you should bring the papers all together. Simply go throughout all rooms in your house and pick up any paper clutter.

- Bring them into one place. Now you have your pile of papers.

- Next, create the folders.

- Then, add labels. For instance, you can make the label named "Bills". Or "Trash". Or "Papers requiring action" (e.g. forms, school papers, etc.)

- Take a handful of papers from the pile. You should make quick decisions: file them right now or trash them. That's it!

179. Solve cable-clutter problem.

Organizing your cables is a never-ending battle. You probably don't want a bunch of cables hanging down there. However, there is a simple trick. Rain gutters are the cheap solutions. Set up your creative cable management under your desk and enjoy! Go to your local home center or hardware store and pick up a rain gutter. You will also need some accessories to install it.

Of course, you can buy a cable organizer and solve the problem easily. Get your cables under control today!

180. A shoe organizer can help you to organize your craft supplies.

You have a huge collection of craft supplies, right? However, they are falling on the floor of your room, they are chucked to the back end. There is a simple trick for that. A plastic Over-the-Door shoe organizer is your solution! It is perfect for storing all these small items.

- Hang a shoe organizer on the door of your room or the closet.

- Put your craft supplies in their seats.

181. Pegboard for your small tools.

You can add a pegboard to your workspace in order to maximize a vertical space. In this way, you will have a quick access to the frequently used tools.

a. First, purchase the pegboard of choice.

b. To take this project to the next level, paint your pegboard in your favorite color.

c. Next, install the pegboard in your workspace.

Installing a pegboard is a quick and inexpensive way to improve your workspace. Keep your workspace safe, organized and beautiful by storing your frequently used tools on your pegboard. Have fun!

182. Keep your craft supplies organized – empty pasta jars.

Your clutter is demanding of you a lot of time and energy. If you feel that you spend too much time reorganizing, cleaning, tidying, dusting and more, your house is probably cluttered. You are aware that your items need to be stored somewhere. If your rooms are crowded and cabinets overflowing, it's time to declutter your space. Otherwise, if that trend continues, you will not be able to bring one more new item in the house.

A little stuff, necessary and unnecessary, create pile and piles of clutter, right? For example, craft supplies. Scissors, glue, pencils, and sharpener, as well as kids' craft supplies can be found all over your house. You can easily keep them well organized with empty pasta jars. It means, clean empty pasta jars and fill them with craft supplies. This solution is completely suitable for small toys, too. Chip and easy!

183. Beauty is in the little things.

"It has long been an axiom of mine that the little things are infinitely the most important." –Arthur Conan Doyle

Small-sized cubby system that can stand on your desks or dresser table is a great idea for organizing your craft and office supplies. You can choose among designs and sizes to keep the clutter under control.

184. Let go of book clutter.

If you are a book addict and love reading every day, you probably face the book clutter. Reading in bed is one of the greatest pleasures for you, but you have too many books and magazines, right? Therefore, it's time to cut the book clutter and get a clean bedroom!

As you probably already know the simplest solution tends to be the best one. You can build the library book cart to organize all your magazines and books. Of course, your mini library can be repositioned to another place in your bedroom. Clever!

185. Create a minimalist wardrobe.

The cluttered closet where your clothes fall on your head when you open it can be a fearful thing. Horror movie. Do you need all these things? Of course, you don't. Therefore, it's time to get rid of them. If something prevents you from taking rid of unwanted things such as emotional reasons, you can help yourself. Of course, you have memories, you spent a lot of money on your clothes, you spent a lot of time, and so on. However, you should focus on quality over quantity and you should focus on the present moment. Where should you start?

- Set aside some time, for instance, on Saturday morning, after family breakfast.

- Take clothes out, empty it into a pile.

- Take a deep breath and start organizing. Don't overthink it.

- Get three large-sized boxes ready. Those are "keep", "maybe", and "toss". Sort everything into these three boxes.

- Take another deep breath and let it go! Experience a true freedom and happiness. Think twice or thrice before buying your next skirt or hat. Just breathe freely!

186. Get rid of unwanted clothes.

If you find that your closet is always overflowing, it's time for cleaning. This is a great hack to get to the root of this problems and start a good declutter. Hang some clothes hangers in the closet "backwards," when using the pointer forcing out toward you. Once you utilize a piece of clothes, add the hanger back to your closet. After about six months, take out clothes that you have not worn. Afterwards, look at what is left. Interesting. Thus, you can remove the pieces of clothing you don't need any more!

187. An easy way to spring-clean your wardrobe.

It is time to remove winter clothes because you will not need it until next season. You can store your winter clothes in a box. You can take a few boxes and label them: sweaters, jackets, scarves, winter hats. Then, organize your spring clothes. You can group your items according to the simple rule "like with like." Group them by sleeve length or color. Be creative and practical.

Keep clothes that really suit you. Get rid of old and outworn clothes. Throw out those old skirts because you don't feel good in them. Get rid of those pants that no longer fit you. Take a special box for items you are donating to charity. It will make you feel better instantly.

188. Three hacks for organizing your wardrobe.

Turn on some good music and start creating the list of what you have in your wardrobe and the list of what you need. Think of all combinations and remove from the list everything that you no longer wear.

a. Why you keep items that make you feel ugly? This creates a heavy vibe and you don't want it. You want a happier and well-organized wardrobe! Therefore, get out of your house all these unwanted pieces of clothing.

b. You can take some classic pieces to a tailor for alterations and create a vintage look.

c. Organize your clothing by type, so that everything is visible. Then, organize by color. For example, sweaters light to dark, long-sleeve tops light to dark and so on. Thus, you will achieve an overall feeling of happiness!

189. Organize your clothing in a vertical fashion.

If you love a mix of vintage clothing and new trendy pieces, this is going to be one of your favorite hacks. This awesome trick allows you to see everything, even vintage clothing from two or more years ago.

Do not lose track of your favorite old clothes. Therefore, simply stack them vertically. You can sort them by colors to ensure the best results!

190. Organize your clothes in a stylized way.

Skip bench seat at the end of the bed or foot rest and use this place as extra space storage. Actually, you can use a low cubby bench to hold your favorite bags, slippers, jeans, sweaters, and other pick-me-ups. And you still will be able to use a flat surface of the storage.

191. Take your closet organization to the next level.

Wire shelf divider is a fantastic invention! Shelf dividers are ideal for creating and maintaining more organized closet. They help support stacked clothing items, so they will help take your closet organization to the next level. You can find wire shelf dividers in a variety of sizes and shapes, so you can choose your style.

They are see-through barriers that are perfect for organizing stacks of your clothing. You will be able to stack your sweaters, blouses and shirts higher than ever before!

192. You get a lot of extra storage with hanging shelves.

There are a lot of things that we use on a daily basis. We just need these items each and every day. Especially if you have kids. Parents are aware of it. However, what to do with this pile of toys, house slippers that are scattered everywhere, socks, everyday accessories that you like to wear most frequently? When it comes to clearing clutter from your bedroom, these things are the first in the list. Are you looking for daily activity organizer? What about hanging shelves? Hanging shelves are inexpensive and practical solutions for tight spaces. They are easy to install because they have hangs from standard closet rods. Very simply. You can find them in popular colors and different sizes depending on their purpose. For example, you will be able to win the battle with clutter in your daughter's room with pink colored hanging shelves. The possibilities are endless.

193. Small space survival – multiple levels of clothing bars!

This clever idea will allow you to keep your tiny closet filled with your up-to-date clothing effectively.

First and foremost, pack off-season clothes in vacuum-sealed bags. Then, maximize closet space by hanging multiple levels of clothing bars!

194. Organize and store all of your sweaters effortlessly.

Do you have a lot of sweaters in a very little closet space? If your sweaters are always scattered everywhere in the closet or stacks of sweaters constantly fall over, here're two simple life hacks.

1) First, fold your sweaters neatly. Folding sweaters properly will significantly save space in your dresser. Therefore, learn a simple folding technique for sweaters. It's easy!

2) Further, you should store them. Be creative or purchase sweater boxes to have peace of mind. Try to find clear boxes so everything will be visible and accessible. The boxes keep your favorite sweaters safe from dust and pests, too. The boxes will make the most efficient usage of space in your dresser or closet.

195. Organize your caps and hats.

If you are a cap addict or you have a collection of well-loved caps, here is a simple hack for keeping your caps and hats tidy and organized. It is really important to get rid of unwanted cups. Consider a question: Do I really think it's worth it to have all these caps in my house? Find a local place to donate them or sell them at garage sale.

Of course, you can store them one inside the other, but there is a better solution to keep them properly. How about simple hooks? And each and every cap, winter cap, baseball cap and hat gets its own place. Many of us like simple solutions without spending too much money and complicated installations, right? Use wardrobe hooks to keep your cap collection organized.

196. Keep your ties well organized.

You can use a wall space to organize items in your wardrobe. If you have a large-sized wall in your closet, it can be a perfect home for your favorite ties. You can arrange a pegboard for this purpose. In this way, you will be able to organize and rearrange your items whenever you want. There is an old rule – Out of sight, out of mind! You should keep your ties organized. Otherwise, you will not be able to see and find all of them. This idea works for hats, shawls, scarves and other items that you can hang. Let your imagination go wild!

197. How to declutter your scarves?

Are your scarves scattered all over your house? Do you waste your time looking for your favorite scarf that matches your red coat? Here're a few steps you should follow and decluttering your scarves will be a breeze.

   a.   Bring everything together. You will get a messy pile.

b. Then, throw out outworn, damaged, and shabby scarves. Get rid of everything you have not worn for the past year. Keep only necessary scarves and purge the rest.

c. Lastly, only store what you will use. Many professional organizers advise us to fold our scarves instead of hanging them. However, it depends on your personal preferences and storage solutions.

198. A storage solution for your scarf collection – hangers.

You can store your scarves creatively. There are a lot of great ways for storing scarves. So choose the way that fits the best into your wardrobe. One of the best ways to store your scarves is to wrap them around hangers. This method makes everything easy to spot. Be creative and enjoy your scarves!

199. The clever concept to store your scarves.

Choose among these creative ways to store your scarf collections. Get inspired and motivated to win your battle with clutter in your closet and bedroom.

a. You can fold or roll your scarves up and store them in a drawer.

b. Try to hang them on command hooks on the back of a door.

c. Then, you can hang them on a towel rod in your closet.

d. Hang shower hooks on a hanger and rearrange your scarves. You can display your scarf collection effectively with this inexpensive trick.

200. Keep your jeans organized.

Are you sentimentally attached to your jeans? Purge your closet following these simple guidelines.

a. **Analyze every individual pair of jeans**. Can you see yourself wearing these jeans? If your answer is NO, get rid of it no matter how stylish or expensive it might look. If your jeans don't make you feel absolutely amazing, get rid of it right now. You can donate them or give them away.

b. **Repairing and repurposing.** Out of sight means less visual clutter, but jeans hidden in the wardrobe tend to be forgotten. Therefore, consider shortening or hemming if you think it'll be worth it. Set aside anything that needs repair and take it to the tailor as soon as possible.

c. **Keep them neat and tidy.** Items like jeans can be much more easily stored by organizing on a shelf. You can sort them by style, color, etc. However, you can choose your favorite method of organizing.

Remember – even if you get rid of all your jeans, you're still you!

201. Keep your skirts neat and tidy.

Start by going through your wardrobe and deciding what skirts you need to get rid of. Try to give away your clothes rather than throw away. You never know who might be able to use your hand-me-downs. After that, you can sort the rest of your skirts. The great way to organize your skirts is to divide them into three zones. Here's how to store all your skirts.

a. **The first zone** is designated for casual everyday skirts. For example, work skirts, beach skirts, etc. This zone should be very accessible.

b. **The second zone** holds skirts that are used weekly or monthly. E.g. elegant and classy skirts for evening outings, fancy clothes skirts, etc.

c. **The third zone** is designated for the skirts that are rarely used.

Getting your closet fresh and well organized is a good first step toward using and enjoying it every day.

202. The best way to store your skirts.

Hang your skirts on hangers with clips. Make sure to fold in the sides so the outside of your skirt will not be marked by the clips. Group your skirts in a way that is logical to you. Take your wardrobe to the next level and use double rods.

203. Life-changing clothing organization tips – dresses.

As you probably already know, the best way to keep your dresses organized is to hang them. Of course, there are a lot of tricks to make it easier.

a. Sort your dresses by outfits; in this way, it's easy to choose something to wear in the morning, something to wear in the evening, etc. You can also group your dresses by color or by length. Simply choose the solution that works for you.

b. It's hard to change dresses if you can't see them. Consider buying decorative garment rack and hang your favorites.

c. To make the best of your closet, consider installing an extendable valet rod.

d. You can use different color hangers for different seasons. Lovely!

204. Life-changing clothing organization tips – tops.

I you have a place in the wardrobe, hang your tops.

Here's an unusual tip: hang all your clothes in the same direction. It sounds crazy, but it will make your life easier. It creates a look of the high level of organization, as well as makes your choice easier.

There is an adage that says, "It's better to donate than accumulate". Therefore, get rid of surplus items and cut the clutter.

205. Life-changing clothing organization tips – jackets and blazers.

a. The first rule is – You can free up a lot of space in your wardrobe by getting rid of unwanted blazers and jackets. Bring your jackets and blazers together and decide: keep or toss. That's it!

b. Hang your jackets and blazers on good-quality wooden hangers. Wire hangers are bad for your jackets.

c. Then, sort them by color. You can also group them by outfits. Therefore, choose the solution that works for you.

206. How to organize your tiny closet?

Small closet presents real storage challenge. However, be inspired and make the most of your cute tiny closet.

a. First and foremost, go through your clothes to get rid of things you don't wear anymore. There is a well-known rule: If you haven't worn some piece of clothing in more than a year, it must go. Divide the items into boxes: give away to charity or toss.

b. Now, it's time to organize your things. It's important to use all of space available to you. You can add a second closet rod, but if you don't want a permanent solution, consider installing a tension rod.

c. Then, consider installing shelves above the closet rod.

d. Space on the back of your closet door is so useful. So install an over-the-door rack.

e. Use multiple-tiered hangers as one of the best space-saving tools. Hang your skirts, blouses, pants, etc.

207. One of the best space saving tools – multi-tiered hangers.

When your tiny closet turns into nightmare closet, you start looking for solutions.

Multi-tiered hangers can provide you with more organizing space than regular hangers. They come as a 3 tier hanger, 4 tier hanger, and a 5 tier hanger. All you need to do is to find the right multi clothes hangers that will transform your closet into an organized haven. How to choose the right tiered hangers?

a. A tiered skirt hanger will provide you with the maximum amount of hanging space for your favorite skirts and cut out the clutter in overstuffed mini closet.

b. Opt for cascade hangers for an easy-to-see look!

c. A swing-arm slack hanger makes it easy to pull your pants or skirts off of the hanger; at the same time, you don't have to take the hanger out of the closet.

d. The more pieces of clothing you have, the more multi-tiered hangers you may need. Choose tiered hangers that make the most sense to you, according to your preferences.

208. Brilliant organization ideas – over-the-door rack.

Tired of searching for an article of clothing in your overstuffed closet?

Over-the-door racks give you maximum storage capabilities. You can hang your bags, scarves, belts, etc. There is also an over-the-door shoe cubby to organize your shoes.

209. Double your closet space.

Here's a perfect solution for your miscellanies – Place a small set of drawers (plastic or wooden) in your overcrowded closet. You can store sewing needles and thread, socks, spare bra straps and other trinkets in these cute drawers. And from now onwards, you will keep your accessories under control. Don't forget to put a full-length mirror for a head-to-toe check. Enjoy!

210. A few life hacks for your tiny closet.

Your tiny closet can be turned into a well-organized space.

a. Simple-to-install wire racks are perfect for streamlining your closet.

b. Then, you can use extra clothing rods, as well as command hooks to keep items organized.

c. Make use of the floor space to store bags, shoes and odds.

Remember – your closet still needs occasional clean-up. Take it under control!

211. Creative solutions for your small closet.

Living in a small house or apartment can have its own advantages, but a small closet isn't one of them. Luckily, you can extend and even double your closet space. Here're the solutions that will blow your mind.

a. You can double your hanging space by adding an extender rod.

b. Double closet space with under shelf baskets and use all the space available to you!

c. If you want to keep the price down, consider this practical solution – Give yourself some extra shelving by hanging a spice rack on your wall next to the closet.

212. Simple hacks to organize your dressing table.

Clutter can really dampen your mood. One day you wake up and realize – your makeup and beauty products have taken over your entire bedroom. Lip glosses and perfumes cluttering up the desk, nail polishes scattered all over the bedside table. And your dresser table is jammed with your beauty stash. If you're looking to streamline your dressing table, follow these four easy steps.

a. Step one: Gather up your products. Therefore, go around your entire bedroom and gather up your beauty items.

b. Step two: check each and every item. Check expiration dates and throw everything that is useless. Get rid of duplicates, too.

c. Step three: dust your table and clean everything in your makeup bags. You can use makeup remover wipes and cosmetic sanitizer wipe as the most convenient solutions.

d. Step four: put beauty products and tools back. Keep them neat and tidy.

In this way, your dresser table will be decluttered and beautiful.

213. Cubby systems are still irreplaceable.

And one of the best tricks to get ship-shape in any corner of your bedroom is to purchase storage cubbies. You can use this simple solution for almost all of your things. It will help you to keep your bedroom tidy and beautiful. You can designate a spot for sports equipment, another spot for bags and backpacks, the third spot for shoes, and so on. Cubby will inspire you to display your favorites, too. The possibilities are endless.

214. Cute and stylish storage.

If you have a large-sized closet, but you need some more ideas for keeping your bedroom in order – add stylish bench system. Canvas cubes inside make a great spot to hold your pick-me-ups. With this versatile solution, you can use flat surface of this bench, too.

215. Be creative – try displaying your favorites.

Don't toss your travel souvenirs or jewelry into a random junk drawer. If you are lacking storage space, why not show off your favorites? It will be the most beautiful décor! Use vertical storage systems and you will get extra space in your bathroom.

216. Organizing jewelry can be challenging.

First and foremost, get rid of anything you don't use a long time. You should throw away anything damaged or dingy. You may be able to repair some pieces of jewelry, especially those that have sentimental value. Then, clean your jewelry thoroughly.

Now it's time to putting things away. Consider picking a ring tree holder to keep your rings handy. Then, arrange your jewelry in your old boxes or purchase some new trendy jewelry displays. There are amazing hacks to organize your necklaces and bracelets such as hanger jewelry holder, necklace stands, jewelry displays, and so on. It's up to you!

217. Organize your jewelry boxes.

Here are a few simple steps to declutter your jewelry box once and for all.

a. Empty your jewelry box or boxes on a table.

b. Can something be tossed out? Throw out any trash. Dump inexpensive chains, cheap and rusty costume jewelry, defunct watches, etc. Then, discard all earrings that have lost their mates. Remove broken jewelry that is not worth repairing. The rest that is worth repairing set aside and take to a jeweler.

c. Next, sort your jewelry into two groups: the jewelry you use every day and the pieces of considerable value. As for the second group, store them in a safe-deposit box.

d. Old jewelry with sentimental associations can be stored separately if possible.

That's it, your jewelry collection should be manageable from now onwards.

218. A stylish way to organize your clutches.

If you are a purse addict, here is a simple hack for keeping your clutches and wallets well-organized. Don't toss your collection of clutches into the dark abyss of a closet. You can keep them one inside the other, but there is a much better solution. How about a kitchen lid rack? And each and every clutch bag gets its own slot. Many of us love these simple solutions to create designated storage and keep things organized.

You can move this rack to the dresser and keep your favorite clutch bags free of dust. Or you can transfer it to a shelf. Anyway, it can be a great decoration for girl's room. So glam!

219. Keep your sunglasses neatly organized.

Your sunglasses are scattered all over your house. There are sunglasses in your purse, on your kitchen table, all over your closet, in dressers, etc. But today's the day!

a. Get rid of broken, chipped and unwanted glasses. Old fashion trends become fresh again, but you cannot save all your items. So it's time to get rid of sunglasses that you wore in high school. You can create the "not sure" pile and consider giving away, donating, or tossing.

b. It's time to store and organize your sunglasses. Here're a few amazing ideas to keep your sunglasses neatly organized.

• Install a small towel rack to hang your eyewear.

• You can use a simple clothes hanger.

• Display your favorites on a beautiful tray. Show your collection with a pride!

You can store your sunglasses in a cute mini basket. You can hang the basket on a wall. So be creative and inspired, the possibilities are endless!

220. Keep your purse neat and tidy.

A huge number of women carry handbags packed with clutter. Makeup, visit cards, old candy wrappers, minty mints, pens, tissues, snacks... There is a simple way to tackle this problem.

1) First, dump out your handbag on the table.

2) Throw out any trash, such as expired membership cards, unwanted photographs, the perfume that's missing the spray bulb. Out!

3) Next, declutter your wallet. Organize your credit cards, phone numbers, and money.

Organize essentials in designated places: cell phone, wallet, keys, notebook and pen, small pack of tissues, lip balm, and hand cream. You can do it!

221. Hang your ironing board.

It is no doubt that the ironing board is taking up too much space in almost every home. This thing always falls on you when you open the closet door. Doesn't that sound familiar? Buy coat hangers at a local store, or use old clothes hangers and hang your bothersome ironing board.

- Measure the length of the ironing board.

- Place two hangers on the wall in the closet. Screw them according to the instructions. Be sure to make them high enough in order to allow the ironing board to hang properly.

- Just hang it up and expand your closet space easily and effortlessly.

LIVING ROOM

Enjoy your clutter-free living room!

Are you embarrassed to let anyone come into your living room? Are you putting other things on hold until you solve the problem with clutter in living room.

Did you know that you can make every corner of your house or apartment useful? Throw away, toss or donate unwanted items. Try to recycle your items and do your part to keep the environment clean. Simplify the clutter and enjoy your relaxing area to the fullest!

222. Organizing hacks for a clutter-free living room.

There is no doubt that even a few extra items can create mess and clutter in your living room, especially if it is tiny space. How to declutter your living room? There are a few basic tips:

Get rid of unwanted items. As you work through the items in your living room, here are two important questions to keep in mind: Is this useful? Is this beautiful? Now throw out any clutter that is laying around. Get rid of surplus furniture, too.

Decide on the purpose. Ask yourself: What is the function of this piece of furniture? Think about what you can sell or donate. You can sell them at garage sale or you can give them away. You should use only the pieces that are necessary for your living room to function. Clean your room thoroughly.

Reorganize your items. Find a spot for each and every item that makes the most sense to you.

It's important to maintain this new clutter-free environment you've created. Once a week, you should take some time to clean this space of dust and dirt. Remember – it gets easier with time!

223. Go a step further.

Magazines, kids' items and office supplies are scattered all over your living room, right? Sick and tired of cleaning and organizing? It seems like a never-ending job. Happily, there are simple life hacks to keep clutter under control.

Step one: Savvy furniture. Try to choose functional furniture that doubles as an extra space storage. For example, a coffee table with a lower shelf or benches with hidden storage

Step two: There is no doubt, the living room is the most frequented room in every house. For that reason, it is a catch-all for clutter! Now, you should remove excess ornaments and plants. During this phase, toss unwanted decoration, threadbare rugs, broken things, and other useless items. Please be practical with every item.

Step three: Think twice before you start purchasing organizers. Is there something else that you can throw away? It's so important to ensure you have enough space storage to organize everything. Remember – less is more!

Now, doesn't that feel better?

224. Simple and traditional living room storage ideas.

Despite the size of your room, you are looking for ideas to save the space and make the room look organized and clutter-free. There are a lot of ways to organize your items in the living room.

- An open shelf is one of the most common pieces of furniture.

- Then, you can use different dressers and sideboards

- Cabinets are irreplaceable when the question is about storage.

- Next solution is lots of cute baskets.

- Display cabinets with their snazzy design are always in vogue.

The possibilities are endless so choose what suits you!

225. Ideas for organizing your open shelving.

Open shelving is a great idea to add some much-needed organization to your living room. Follow these simple rules and you will keep your living room shipshape.

a. **Preparation.** First and foremost, make sure you'll have enough space. If you are not sure, consider buying adjustable shelving.

b. **Categorization.** Group items by category. Put like with like.

c. **Imagination.** Invest in good containers such as decorative wire baskets or vintage buckets. Let your imagination run wild!

d. **Presentation.** Display your favorites like family heirlooms and photographs. However, be careful not to overcrowd your shelves.

226. A cozy living room makeover – dressers.

A dresser serves as a perfect closet alternative or as an ideal supplemental living room storage. How to organize your dresser? Here are a few rules.

Free up your space. Get a jump start on your dresser. As you work through the items on your dresser, keep in mind this question: Is this useful? Then, throw out any clutter.

Decide on the purpose. Ask yourself: What is the function of this dresser? For example, if you're lacking wardrobe space, you can store your clothes here. Or your dresser will hold items that you use every day. It's up to you.

Dresser is one of the best storage solutions for the living room so that you'll be able to simplify the clutter and enjoy your relaxing area to the fullest.

227. Cut clutter in the living room closet.

Is your closet in the living room jammed with clutter? If you are struggling with clutter in your closet, you are not alone. Luckily, with the right setup, you will find a place for each and every item. Take everything out of the closet. Work systematically around the entire space. Ready, set, go!

Create three piles:

    a.   Stuff that shouldn't go in the closet;

b. Items that should go in the closet;

c. Clutter and garbage.

Follow these few steps and you will declutter your closet easily and effortlessly. After decluttering, you should sort your items one by one.

228. Keep living room closet well organized.

Keep the clutter down by organizing all your necessities in a closet.

a. After decluttering, you should organize the living room closet according to your preferences. Ask yourself: What is the function of this closet?

b. Living room is definitely an area where the closet is a big help. You can choose long narrow closet to maximize space in your living room.

c. There are so many brilliant ideas to maximize closet space. Remember to use hangers with clips, multiple & tiered hangers, hooks, baskets, and other great solutions to keep your closet neat and tidy.

This versatile storage can hold all kinds of items, from your coats to yoga pants. If you still need a space storage, a console cabinet is a perfect solution for your essentials.

229. You get a lot of extra storage with hanging shelves.

There are a lot of necessities that make our living room looks messy. Especially if we have kids. However, what to do with this pile of newspapers, books, toys, snacks and other items that are scattered all over your living room?

What about floating shelves?! Floating shelves are inexpensive and practical solutions for your living room. Floating shelves are easy to install so you will get an extra storage without taking up floor space. You can find them in popular colors and different sizes to fit within your living room. Good luck!

230. Floating shelves – decorative and functional ideas.

Decorative and functional floating shelves can be mounted on nearly any wall in your living room. They offer you plenty of accessorizing options. These amazing shelves can be grouped or stacked so you will get an extra storage and space to display your favorites. Floating shelves cut clutter and add style to your living room at the same time. Here's a practical idea to organize your house plants.

Arrange your house plants on floating shelves and you will get an elegant and chic decorative detail. They are easy to maintain versatile storage options for you. Make functional and beautiful living room!

231. Be practical but chic!

It's a great idea to use a combination of open shelves and cupboards. In this way, you can display your favorites and conceal clutter. Therefore, select smart and savvy storage units to ensure everything is put back in place. Choose from a huge number of brands, designs and colors and enjoy your relaxing environment.

232. Get the right coffee table.

To get an extra space storage in your living room, you can purchase a coffee table with built-in storage. You can get the table with either an open shelf storage or shelf drawers. Drawers can conceal all sorts of necessities such as remotes, books magazines, and coasters, so you will be able to turn a simple table into a great storage.

233. Organize your coffee table.

How about decluttering your living room? You can start from a coffee table. Do you have the coffee table jammed with clutter? Does anything belong in another room? Can something be tossed out?

Your coffee table in the living room is perfect for items that are apt to be used frequently. But usually, it is cluttered with a wide variety of items. However, you can make the most of your storage options. Clean your coffee table and clear clutter out of drawers. Now you can use it for the stack of your favorite magazines, the books, coasters, candle holder, etc. Anyway, try to keep this storage spot organized.

234. Dress up your coffee table.

Sick and tired of clutter on your coffee table? Books, newspapers, remote controls, pencils, toys... Retake the valuable surface of your coffee table with this simple hack. Place a nice tray on your table to corral small items. In this way, you will discourage placing all sorts of things on your coffee table because they already have their home. Easy.

235. Cute nesting tables – the solution for a small living room.

It serves as a multi-tiered coffee table in your living room. It is easy to move piece of furniture and it provides you with more capabilities than open coffee tables. They are perfect for small living rooms because they take up less space.

They come in sets of two or three, so you get an extra tabletop surface as needed.

236. Old-fashioned ottoman.

This is an excellent storage furniture because it can conceal a large number of items. Ottoman comes in a variety of styles, designs, sizes, and colors, so you can bring organization to your living room in a stylish way.

Remove the lid and you can store anything from blankets to toys.

237. Built-Ins - maximize space in your living room.

Built-ins will give your living room a well-organized appearance. You can frame your doorway with shelves and add amazing storage to your living room. You can organize your books or display your favorite collection.

Built-ins can turn an unused space in the living room into a multi-functional storage. You can use irregularly shaped walls and nooks. Make the most of your small living room!

238. Just imagine – storage bench!

Use your imagination and visualize two functions into one. Yes, it is a storage bench! It provides a place to sit, and cubbies below can be used for bins. This is a real space saver. Corral kids' toys, craft supplies, and other trinkets and conceal them under your bench. You can choose from designs and styles and your living room will get a stylish and well-organized appearance.

239. Organize your favorites – collectible figurines.

It's time to find the right home for your collectibles. Display them and add an artistic touch to your walls.

Floating shelves are a savvy solution for your favorite collectibles. In this way, you will get a stunning home décor that declutters and stores at the same time.

240. Rolling cart in your living room.

The rolling cart is an especially good idea for a small living room. If you need an extra counter space, consider buying a cart.

A small rolling bar cart is just what you need to make things more manageable. And you can place your cart anywhere you want. It can serve as a good home for your house plants.

241. Tackle kids' belongings.

If your children use coffee table for board games and drawing, no big deal. Teach them to clear the supplies off coffee table after each usage. Then, they should store their belongings at the place designated. Gather small items such as toy bricks and blocks, pencils and kids craft supplies and conceal them. Nevertheless, the best solution is to set up desks or work table for those activities. However, if you don't have a space for an additional furniture, use stylish canvas storage bins and declutter your living room. It is a great solution when you are in a hurry.

242. Dining room organizations – baskets.

If you find you can't use your living room for what it meant to do because of certain reasons, it's time to solve this problem. This is the area where the family can socialize with one another. Your living room is a perfect place for gatherings with family and friends. However, if your living room is jammed with stuff, it cannot serve its purpose.

If your living room is filled with knick-knacks, consider buying pretty straw baskets. Baskets are great organization tools for living room. You can keep lots different things in them. Remove clutter from your coffee table, armchairs, and floor. You can go one step further and purchase the baskets with handles to hang them on a wall using hooks.

243. Creative storage ideas for a small living room.

After decluttering your home, you realize – there are lots of items of sentimental value to you! If you would like to save the items of great importance to you, you should find them a "home" in your "home". It can be your living room.

Install small rectangular shelf for open storage, and clear off the floor in your living room. Display your favorites such as the books, and things of great importance like antiques and heirloom.

244. Creative organization solutions – freestanding cabinets.

If you are looking for a stylish way to organize your home, consider installing freestanding cabinets. This amazing furniture can be used to separate living room from the rest of the house. It also provides you with a large amount of storage.

245. Burlap buckets as clever organizers.

How about stylish burlap-covered buckets? You can use them to hold odds, crafts, and other necessities. Then, hang them on the wall and get clutter-free environment!

Apart from photographs and paintings, you can hang your favorite collections on the wall. You can also purchase a stylish ottoman with space storage and hide your burlap baskets there.

246. A single drawer file cabinet.

A mini filing cabinet will not take a lot of space in your living room but it is incredibly practical. It serves as a storage for your files and documents, as well as a side table. Use its surface to showcase your decoration or use it as a mini coffee table. It is a simple solution to conceal clutter when you are in a hurry. Your discreet cabinet still needs occasional clean-up, so get rid of excess items from time to time.

247. Put furniture to work – console table.

Multipurpose furniture is a must-have in your small living room. Choose the furniture with moving parts and storage space, so you will save space and cut clutter at the same time. Consider buying a console table and add style to your living room.

Trendy baskets can be lined up beneath for an extra space storage.

248. Add glam with narrow shelves.

Add style and glamour to your home with narrow shelves. They are perfect for easy access to the things you use every day in your living room. Remember – any unused space is a great spot for storage space! Don't neglect the corners because they are the perfect place for those shelves. Small narrow shelves will provide you with just enough space for your everyday items, as well as beautiful display space for your collectables.

249. Traditional hutches and armoires.

Tackle the clutter problem with these old-fashioned pieces of furniture.

Don't go out and shop for some storage pieces before you sort through your living room. If you have an old armoire jammed with clutter, consider repairing and you will get a lot of extra space for storage.

Hutches and armoires provide you with plenty of concealed storage for organizing your items.

250. A simple hack – cute decorative trays.

Opt for decorative trays to keep organized small items and necessities that you use on a daily basis. Find "home" for your eyewear, small toys, pencil, book, crafts, office supplies, etc. Here is a brilliant idea: each family member can be assigned a tray for holding everyday items.

251. Pro organizer trick – a table skirt.

Here's an opportunity to express your creativity! Choose stylish table skirt to hide your organization storage under table. Therefore, corral your necessities and put them in the baskets. Then, hide your baskets behind the table skirt. So glam.

252. Organize your mini bar.

For this purpose, you can find a metal cart with glass and bottle support. It is just what you need to make things a lot easier. When you're hosting a party, use your rolling cart. Simply move the whole station all over your living room.

253. The clever ideas to make the most of your space in living room.

Your home entertainment center probably consists of TV set, DVD/CD player, sound system, the collection of DVDs and CDs, etc. And all these items can create a disorganized jumble.

You can save floor space by installing a flat panel, wall-mounted television.

If you have an older TV set, tuck it into a television cabinet or an armoire.

An armoire can also provide extra storage space in your living room. It is a great idea for small apartments. So keep it in mind and think twice before getting rid of your old armoire.

254. Organize books according to your style.

If you are a big fan of books, you can face the problem with too many books and a lack of shelves. Too many books create too much clutter in your house. Drawers wouldn't shut, shelves are full and old books could be found in every room. Book, books, book… So you finally realize, it's time to let go of some of them.

The advice is simple – remove the excess and set yourself free!

There is no doubt, it is a large project, but it is important to start from somewhere.

a. First of all, you must get rid of some books. What can you do with your old and unwanted books? You can sell these books online or donate them to the local library.

b. Now dust the shelves and the books. You can use a vacuum cleaner for some of the books.

c. Next logical step, sort your books by genre or author. You can also arrange them by the frequency of use. It's totally up to you. The books should be nice and neatly sorted and easily accessible.

d. Keep in mind that you can store over thousands of books on your e-reader.

Keep your books organized from now onwards; enjoy reading!

255. Cut the book clutter with stylish bookcases.

A stylish bookcase is one of the best ways to keep your books neatly organized. They are perfect for storing magazines, ornaments, family photographs, and other accessories.

You can go one step further and use bookends and magazine holders.

Use fabric-covered box files for storing day-to-day paperwork.

256. Prevent magazine clutter.

Are your floor and tabletops cluttered with magazines? Or your magazines are stacked in piles in a corner of your living room? It's time to cut that clutter once and for all! Here are a few steps to clear clutter and get organized.

Step one: Bring all your magazines together.

Step two: Have a trash bag on hand and toss unwanted magazines. Dispose of everything that you haven't used in the last year and you will never use again. Try to recycle your magazines and do your part to keep the environment clean.

Step three: Decide which magazines you need to keep. If your answer is – "I probably should read", get them out of your house. If you need to read some magazines for work assignment or your kids need some of them for school, you can keep them.

Step four: Sort and organize your magazines.

257. Keep your magazines neatly organized (Part I).

You love your magazines so much. However, do you have magazine holders? Or do you have a special home for them, for example, on a bookshelf? If your answer is No, it's time to sort your favorites. Here are a few ideas to do that easily and effortlessly.

a. Therefore, you should organize them and put them at the place designated. A good solution is to purchase a couple of magazine racks.

b. Go to your local store and pick a stylish magazine holder. Display your magazines in the living room and delight your guests who love to read magazines.

c. Vertical spine bookcase is a great idea if you have a huge collection of magazines; in this way, you can group them by category.

Enjoy your clutter-free living room!

258. Keep your magazines neatly organized (Part II).

There are a lot of extraordinary ways to sort your magazines.

a. A stylish crate on wheels is a great way to organize your magazines.

b. Consider hanging decorative buckets and bins and find a perfect home for your favorite magazine collections.

c. You can opt for an over-the-door magazine storage pockets.

You can use these ideas to organize all your ripped out magazine pages, too. Good luck!

259. Organize your comic book collection.

a. You should place your comics in protective bags to keep them safe from dirt and spills. These bags come in three most common materials: polyethylene, mylar, and polypropylene.

b. Then, organize your comics in the right boxes. It's good to find acid-free boxes. You could organize them by series or by the publisher, it's up to you. Consider buying a comic notebook as a perfect solution for your favorites.

c. After that, you should find a storage spot for your collectables.

260. Make a better visual impression – hide electronics.

Sometimes, even a few essential tech pieces can make clutter. For that reason, keeping your living room tidy and organized can be challenging. Especially if you own a small living space.

You can tuck your scanner or printer into the drawers and cut clutter once and for all.

261. Cubbies in your living room.

Cubbies are ideal furniture for living room. They are easy to manage and rearrange. Cubbies are great for storage and display. How to declutter your cubby system? Follow a few simple steps.

a. Take everything out and lay it on the ground.

b. Throw out, donate or recycle everything that is useless.

c. Wipe down your cubbies.

d. Reorganize your items by categories. Use baskets if needed to keep everything neat and tidy.

Organize your collectables, photographs, figurines, books and other favorites once and for all.

262. Home office in your living room.

You can set up your home office inside a closet in your living room. And you will get plenty of storage space. With the door closed, nobody know your home office was there. Clever.

263. A great solution for extra storage in your living room.

You can frame your sofa with custom cubbies that will provide you with extra space storage.

First and foremost, get rid of all unwanted items to free up space for necessities. Then, arrange your items grouping them by categories.

You can install a mix of open and closed storage. In that way, you can display your favorites and hide some items. Make the most of your living room with this savvy design solution!

264. The simplicity and beauty – floor bins.

Tired of blankets, plush toys, pillows and other clutter in your living room? Eliminate clutter and beautify your room with this clever storage solution. Consider buying floor bins. They come in different sizes and patterns so you can match your décor. These floor bins are cute and attractive, so you can easily teach your kids to pick up after themselves!

265. How to throw a party in a small living room?

You have a small living room, but you love throwing parties. Don't let a small space hold you back! Be creative and use your space in a unique way. Prevent excess clutter during the party and keep everything under control.

a. **Rearrange your furniture.** A living room with the furniture moved out of the way can make a great space for your party.

b. **A creative mindset.** In terms of seating plan, you should be creative. You can use folding chairs, poufs, pillows, etc.

c. **Buffet style.** Serve appetizers on large platters and arrange them on your coffee table and other countertops. You can serve beverages on stylish rolling carts. Try to utilize every available surface such as a console and shelves.

Choose the right lighting, throw a smile, and you will throw the most glamorous party ever!

266. Organizing your recordings (I).

The most households have considerable libraries of CDs, DVDs, and other

recordings. Organizing these items can be challenging.

a. It is the best to alphabetically group the films by title and the music by artist.

b. It's the most convenient to place your recordings on a shelf specifically meant for them. These shelves won't take up your space too much.

c. If you collect VHS tapes, you had better label all of those tapes before they create a clutter nightmare.

d. In terms of DVD library, the best advice you ever got is – Borrow it, don't buy it! So, you can rent movies instead of buying them.

e. As your musical taste changes, your old CDs can create a lot of clutter. You can sell them on the Internet. Do a search for "sell CDs" or "Used CDs," and you will find specialized websites.

267. Organizing your recordings (II).

Thanks to technological progress and advances, recordings have been improved by digitization. For example, digital video recorders use a hard drive to store a lot of hours of programming. MP3s are revolutionizing the storage of music. Compressed digital music files significantly save our home space. Now we can store thousands of songs on a small device.

DVD burners can record programming on thin DVDs, and they take up far less space than videotapes. The files should be backed up from time to time and that's it!

The clutter-cutting benefits are obvious!

268. Velcro – organize your remote controls.

There are too many remote controls nowadays. One remote control for DVD player, the second one for TV, the third one for an air conditioner, and so on. Consider attaching Velcro on the wall and on the back of your remote control. You can organize your gamepads in the same way.

269. How to maintain a decluttered living room?

Your clutter defines a part of you as a person. For example, if you love collectibles or books, these things reflect your passion. However, you should be organized. How to maintain decluttered living room?

a. Try to spend ten minutes each evening clearing out everything that doesn't belong in your living room.

b. Then, each time you plan to buy something new for your living room, search through your drawers and cabinets so you do not buy duplicates.

c. It is important to sort through your cabinets and drawers at the start of each season.

CHILDREN'S ROOM

"Cut clutter game"

It's time to let go of past and make space for new memories. Before you start decluttering kids' room, sit down and try to explain the organization process to them. Stick to simplicity. Decluttering and organizing are best shown by example. Let's play the "Cut clutter game"!

270. Declutter kids' rooms – well begun is half done!

While the same basic rules for decluttering apply when you organize children's room, there are some small differences and the additional considerations. How to begin?

a. First and foremost, you should involve your kids in the process of decluttering their rooms. The primary and the most important goal is to teach them how to care for their things.

b. Before you start decluttering, sit down and try to explain the organization process to them. They should understand basics, so stick to simplicity. Everything else will be described during the process. Decluttering and organizing are best shown by example.

c. Make space for children's questions. If children understand what is expected of them, they will be much more cooperative.

271. Let's play the "Cut clutter game"!

This is a special challenge for you. And for your kids, too. After explaining of the decluttering process, go from intention to realization. Here is a step-by-step guide for decluttering children's room.

a. **Toss and put away:** Use trash and recycle boxes or bags. Toss everything that are missing important parts or that are broken. You should decide together with your kids. You can create the "not sure" box but decide as soon as possible.

b. **Cleaning:** Use this opportunity to dust, vacuum and wipe down furniture. It's a good idea to involve your kids in cleaning their room.

c. **Divide and conquer:** To achieve the best results, you can divide children's room into several main zones. These are 1) the sleeping zone, 2) study zone, 3) the entertaining zone, and 4) the grooming zone.

272. Declutter kid's room – surplus furniture.

If kid's room is jammed with surplus furniture, it's time to declutter. Having too many tables, baskets, kids tabourets, and other things make the room appear smaller.

    a. Get rid of surplus furniture Think what will stay and what will go. You can sell them at the garage sale or you can donate them. The same basic rule for decluttering applies here – less is more!

    b. The way you arrange furniture can make a big difference. Find a spot for each and every piece that makes the most sense to you.

273. How to declutter children's bedroom?

Toss it or keep it. While you are going through the room, ask yourself: "Do my kids really need all these things in the bedroom?" and "Is anything in their sleeping area unused?". Remember to ask: "What's important to my child?". Then, toss unwanted items.

Keep it simple. Make six piles together with your kids – "keep", "put away in another place", "give away", "sell", "trash", and "recycle (repurpose)".

Sort. It is important to designate a spot for each and every item. Put items back in their places.

274. Buy organizing products by considering the bigger picture.

After dividing kids room into zones, you have to set up certain spots for certain items. What to do next? Of course, you should buy organizers. You can also make them yourself. Just make sure to purchase organizers that match the décor of kids' room. It is important to consider the aesthetics. If you have no idea what to purchase and find this difficult, stick to a well-known rule – The simpler, the better!

275. Organize a comfortable sleeping area.

It's so easy to let a child's room turn chaotic; moreover, most people have a small child's bedroom. It's important to declutter bed and under bed space periodically.

a. Pick all the garbage off the floor and throw it away. Remove all items that don't belong in kids' bedroom.

b. You should only have pillows and one soft toy on the child' bed.

c. Then, declutter a bedside table. Free up space for necessities such as a glass of water, a lamp, and maybe a magazine or a book. Consider buying a bedside table with drawers so your child will be able to put necessities back. In this way, you will keep it from getting too messy.

276. Maintain kids' room.

To maintain your fresh and uncluttered environment, stick to a few basic rules:

a. Make beds every morning.

b. Keep kids' clothing organized. Place them in the closet or the laundry basket.

c. Take control of bedside clutter. Make sure kids don't ruin what you have achieved.

277. Organize kids' study space.

Tired of messy kids' desk? By decluttering and organizing kids' study space, you'll feel less stressed and your house will be well organized.

You will need two basic things: 1) a child-friendly desk, 2) a storage space for school and craft supplies.

1) **Kid's desk** serves as a homework station, as well as a craft area. Therefore, make sure they have a good-sized and uncluttered work surface. Throw away everything that is useless. Divide into sections to make decluttering easier. For example, declutter and sort items in only one drawer. Do not go on until you have finished that job. Then, choose

another drawer or shelf, and so on. Rome wasn't built in a day!

2) **Storage solution** is a very important issue for your overall organization. So, make sure to provide your kids with enough storage space. Choose from different drawers, cabinets, baskets, bins and other storage solutions according to your needs. This makes it easier for kids to pick out their items.

278. Use desktop and drawer organizers.

Is kids' desk cluttered with papers, pens, rulers, notebooks and other items? Do you want to help your kids bring order to their homework station? The solution is simple – use desktop and drawer organizers. Your kids can divide their items and group them into categories for better organization results. Choose from different designs, patterns, and sizes and create a wonderful space for studying and creative activities.

279. Organize kids' study area– cube shelves.

Conquer wasted space with amazing cube shelves for the wall that your little ones will love. Choose from a variety of colors and sizes, adorn your walls, and help your kids get organized.

In terms of materials, opt for see-through acrylic to make things more manageable. Clear the desk of clutter and delight your little ones!

280. Organize kids' study area – floating shelves.

Floating shelves are a fun and unique storage space for kids. It is very important that kids can display their favorites on these shelves. Floating shelves will help you to maintain order in kid's rooms.

Floating shelves can hold artwork, books, collectible figures, photographs, and other necessities. The possibilities are endless!

281. 2-in-1 organizer – pegboard shelving system.

If your children need a little extra encouragement to declutter their own space, you have to find a creative and clever solution. Pegboard shelving system is a cute and clever room organizer that your little ones will love.

Attach the shelves to the wall so that the children can reach them easily. These shelves will inspire your kids to keep their room well organized. They offer the opportunities for creativity and you can customize them according to your needs. Get a spotless and beautiful kid's room!

282. A savvy solution for small items.

If kids' room is jammed with tons of clutter, transparent containers make your life easier! Transparent containers are practical because they offer an easy visibility of items. They are perfect for storing small items such as craft supplies and school supplies. You can stack your new containers and save space in kids' room.

If you are switching small items into new containers, try to maintain clutter-free area with a few easy tricks. Designate a spot for each category. For example, designate a box for crayons; then, label that box. Next, designate a box for watercolors, and so on. These transparent containers can hold anything. Kids will love them!

283. Quick ideas for organizing crafts supplies.

Install a peg rack on the back of a closet door for an extra space storage. It can hold tools such ribbons, spools of thread, and so on. This trick will free up kids' space for work so that kids can neatly store their crafts supplies.

284. One of the best ways to declutter craft supplies.

There are a lot of ideas to organize kids' small items. Cabinet with drawers is one of the best storage solutions. The items are grouped into categories and sorted in designated spots.

You can label the drawers; then, add dividers to the drawers to bring order to whole space.

285. Use recycled storage – "monkey see, monkey do" method.

Your little ones learn by the "monkey see, monkey do" method. So you have to set a good example. Teach your child that he/she doesn't need stuff to be happy. Find a creative, cheap and fun way to stash and organize these necessities.

Watercolor pens, pom poms, feathers, and other items are scattered all over the desk. Use empty coffee cans to store crafting items and declutter work area. Simply wrap these cans in a decorative paper of choice and arrange them on kids' desk. Kids will be delighted! You can also repurpose old galvanized buckets.

286. Repurpose items for organization and storage.

A wire shower caddy can be a great spot for crafts supplies. Hang a caddy on the wall and organize notebooks, scissors, pencil holders, and other necessities. Just make sure it is low enough for little hands to reach.

287. Declutter craft supplies – shoe organizer.

The way you organize kids' craft supplies plays a big part in making a clean and tidy room. If you want to save money and declutter kids' room at the same time, use a shoe organizer!

It will hold almost all of craft items.

Make sure to choose transparent shoe organizer, so kids can easily reach desired items. Invite your kids to join you and group all items into categories. Remember – when you free yourself from clutter you have much more to give to the things that really matter in your life.

288. Quick and clever idea – pegboard.

Pegboard is an ideal contrivance for storing kids' crafts supplies. Paint the pegboard and hang it above kids' desk. Just make sure it is low enough for your little ones to reach.

Kids will be inspired because they will have everything visible and accessible.

289. Small cubbies – storage and display.

Whether you want to organize toys, craft supplies, or something else, small cubbies are always a great idea for kids' room. They are easy to manage and rearrange. Follow these simple steps to declutter and reorganize your cubby storage.

a. Take everything out and lay it on the ground.

b. Throw out everything that is useless.

c. Wipe down your cubbies.

d. Reorganize and group craft supplies by categories. Use cans, bins or baskets to keep everything neat and tidy.

It will be the great display for kids' artwork, too.

290. Display kids' artwork.

There are a lot of nifty ways to display your child's masterpieces. Here're some unique solutions for displaying your child's art.

* You can hang them using clothespins that are attached to a strip of wood.

- Consider using picture frames and display them on a wall.

- A chalkboard is always good idea to keep your wall clean.

- Clipboard display is one of the simplest solutions ever.

291. How to combat book clutter?

Decluttering kids' books can be a challenging task, but with the right plan you will get them well organized.

Bring all books together.

Toss or donate. Toss everything you no longer use. Get rid of damaged books. Consider donating books that children will never read.

Keep. Keep current reference books and books of great financial value. Keep books of great sentimental value, too.

Sort and organize. Designate a spot in kids' room for their books. Invest in a good bookshelf because the number of books will increase over the years. You can sort books in a manner that is logical to you. You can alphabetize kids' books to make them easier to find desired books.

292. Choose the appropriate storage.

Now, kids' room is under control. Relatively. But half a loaf is better than none! So, be careful. If your children go back to their old habits, toys, clothing and papers are likely to start piling up again. Of course, you don't want that to happen! Therefore, you have to devote some time to your little ones, teaching them to follow good habits. You can teach your child that each and every item has a "home".

Your little ones learn by example and they want to be involved. Therefore, allow them to choose the "home" for their favorite books. Ask your child to help you select the right storage space. It is important that this storage should make sense for your child, not for you. Thus, your child will learn basic organizing skills.

293. Keep kids' books neatly organized – wall book bin.

Wall book bin is designed to be attached directly to the wall next to the desk. It can hold not only books but also magazines, comic books, folders, binders, etc. This is a simple and kid-friendly way to get kids' necessities well organized. You can install a few book bins and sort the books by categories. Cute.

294. A great idea to organize and store kids' books.

There are a lot of inexpensive and practical ways to organize books in kids' room. One of the most creative ideas is built-in bookshelves! You can use cheap and available materials and build amazing storage space for kids' books. If you tend to avoid custom-made shelves and you are planning to make your own DIY shelves to match décor – consider creating built-in bookshelves. Good luck!

295. Life hacks for tiny room – corner bookcase.

This handy solution will save space in a tiny kids' room. The corner bookcase will maximize space while offering enough storage space for books. You can find them in popular colors and different sizes to fit into décor.

Your kids will have a quick and easy access to the frequently used school books, comic books or picture books.

296. Go one step further – a container with wheels!

You are doing very well for now! So keep up the good work! It's time to take the organization on kids' room to the next level.

When everything has its own spot, your child can find what he/she is looking for quickly and easily. Consider purchasing the containers with wheels as a storage for small items. This fun kids' storage solution will cut clutter and help your child keep bedroom neat and tidy. In this way, you will teach your child to care for her/his belongings. At the same time, your child will have fun. Make it work for you!

297. Organize kids' toys – basics.

Toys. You feel like they are everywhere in your house. On the kitchen table, on the shelves, in bathroom, in your bed, everywhere on the floor... But toys are super funny! However, what to do?

1) **Donation and garage sell.** Try your best to minimize the number of toys in your house. Be convinced that less is better and always choose quality over quantity. Find a local place to donate. If you want to have a garage sale when you are finished this job, plan the date right now. Planning garage sale will give you an additional motivation to stay on target and finish this a time-consuming task on time. It will also help you to prepare for your garage sale (for example, invite families and friends to join you, advertise it in a local paper, and so on).

2) **Toss and give away.** It's time to start throwing out the unwanted toys. Discard the things that are stained, broken, missing some parts, etc. You have to get rid of

things that are no longer age appropriate, too. Of course, you can't give away items that aren't useful to anyone.

3) **Storage.** After that, you should find a convenient place to store kids' toys. Keep the toys in the baskets, closet, or storage boxes. It's up to you. Teach your kids to love the uncluttered look.

298. Let go of sentimental toys.

Did you spend your hard-earned money on insanely expensive toys? After a while, they are broken or missing some important parts. Or they are no longer age appropriate. How to know when to throw some toys away or donate them to charity?

You can divide these toys into following categories:

- Children haven't used it in the last year;

- You can create" they would never use that" list;

- These toys are too old;

- They are broken and completely useless;

- You have duplicates.

You will find that you enjoy being in your home and kids room, and you'll spend less time maintaining and cleaning your home. Set yourself free!

299. A simple plan to declutter the toys.

If you struggle with toy clutter, come up with an efficient toy-organizing plan and you will get all toys under control once and for all.

Focus. First and foremost, try to focus on one area of kids' room at a time. Apply simple rule named "only one activity at a time" and avoid being distracted. For example, focus on under bed storage. Gather all of the toys into bed.

Keep track of the toys. Next, you should designate a spot for each and every toy, without exception. You can add labels and take this task to the next level. Therefore, from now on, when your child wants to play with certain toy, he/she will always know where it is.

300. Store and simplify.

Here's a great tip for simplifying kids' bedroom.

Consider buying beds that come with storage options. Built in, drawers and shelves are perfect solutions for kids' room. Kids' items can be tucked away underneath the bed, while everyday necessities can be at arm's reach. Of course, bring your little ones into the process and ask them for their opinion.

301. It's time to get organized – built-in shelving systems.

It's a fact – accumulating toys is much easier than giving them away. Decluttering toys can be tricky, but you can get them into ship-shape for sure. You only need enough storage space and good clever plan to store your items.

Try to use every inch of available space in child's room with built-in shelving systems. The lower shelves can be used for small toys and favorites while the upper shelves can display artwork and collectibles.

302. Corner cubby system – you're ready to get organized!

Make advantage of every corner of kids' playroom using simple cubby system. Corral toys and other small playthings in wicker baskets; then, put them into your cubby storage. Open cubbies are perfect storage and display for different games, plush toys, artwork, etc. Choose from different colors and styles to coordinate your cubby system with your existing furnishings. Teach your kids the value of the right organization and beautiful room!

303. A clutter-free life – look for double-duty solutions!

Look for double-duty solutions and you will get children's room in order! For example, consider buying a cute storage bench with drawers. Choose from different sizes, designs and colors to fit a room's décor. Now you can sort all toys by style or color.

You will need a little bit of organization to put every misplaced item into its designated spot. After that, your life will be much easier!

304. Choose the right toy box.

Toy box provides kids' playroom with a plenty of storage. Toy box is one of the best options if you don't have enough space in children's room. It doubles as a bench for an additional seating and it can be repositioned everywhere.

The toy boxes are made of sturdy material and they come with safety hinge. You can choose from colors and designs to delight your kids and cut toy clutter once and for all.

305. Use old baskets to keep toys off the floor.

A basket is a great solution for kid's toys because you can organize them very quickly. Pick the toys and just load up the basket. It would be even old laundry basket, it does not matter You can also teach your kids to declutter the entire room, playing at the same time. It will be their fun activity! However, you should set an example for your children. They always learn more from example than words. Take the basket and give another basket to your child. You will be surprised with the results!

306. Clever toy storage trick – hidden buckets.

Place the buckets filled with toys in the inner storage of your ottoman. You can use plastic buckets, galvanised buckets or the other toy storage bins and enjoy this uncluttered look. You can choose designs and colors. You can also stack up small buckets and keep them together with zip ties. In terms of outdoor toys, the same principle applies to them. Put metal buckets into your mudroom closet. You can use labels and take the organization to the next level. Enjoy this practical solution for toy messes!

307. Store kid's puzzle pieces.

You totally understand this never-ending process of organizing and storing kids' puzzles. If they lose a certain part of them, the toy becomes useless. You can use zipper pencil pouches. Further, you can store all of the pouches in one of your bins. It makes it easy to grab a certain zipper pouch. In that way, the puzzles will be easily accessible for your little ones. In addition to this solution, you can use a gallon zip top bag for puzzle pieces.

308. Simple solutions for the favorite puzzles.

To keep puzzle pieces neatly organized, grab some lidded containers; then, organize each puzzle to a separate box. Then, cut out the picture of the completed puzzle and tape it to the lid. Brilliant idea!

309. Some more organizing ideas for kids.

This life hack will help you to declutter kid's room cheap and easy. You can reuse an old wooden crate as an additional storage space for kids' stuff. Paint it and add wheels to the bottom if desired. Fill this vintage crate with kids' favorite toys. It's great idea to fill it with toys that kids use everyday

The wheeled crate offers the advantage of being easily moved. They are ideal for a cramped space because they can easily be repositioned. You will free up space in the room and your kids will be happy!

310. A totally clever idea for car toys.

Corral all toy vehicles once and for all. If you have a few dozen car toys, and you want to organize them and display your collection, the clutter will be gone in fifteen minutes! With this clever idea, you will have a convenient place to store the collection of car toys.

Use a magnetic knife strip for storing and displaying car toys. This is a kind of bar that is typically used for knives. Install the magnetic strip in a child's bedroom and organize toys by color, by size, etc. Of course, ask your son for help. Be creative and enjoy!

311. Use a shoe organizer to declutter small toys.

You can organize children's items right now. If you don't want to spend your money on new baskets, bins and other organizers, use a shoe organizer to hold all kids' plastic dolls. This idea works for plastic animals, small balls, marbles, play mobiles, fast food toys, etc. There is a rule — out of sight, out of mind! Make sure to choose transparent shoe organizer, so kids can easily reach the toys.

    a.   First, bring all small toys together.

b. Then, go through these toys, getting rid of everything that missing parts and that are broken.

c. Invite your kids to join you and help you to choose which things to give away and which things they would like to keep.

d. Clean a shoe organizer properly.

e. Then, put plastic toys into this amazing organizer. You and your kids can group all items into categories. Anyway, this solution will give your kids more space to play in their room.

312. Garden baskets for plush toys and stuffed animals.

Keep kid's favorite plush toys in one place with this great idea. Simply hang garden baskets on a wall. Make sure to hang them at a low height so your little ones can reach them and put them back easily. Teach your children to love the uncluttered look. It's a lovely look!

This clutter is demanding of you a lot of hard-earned money. Help your kids declutter their stuff. There is one more important tip for you – begin buying fewer toys and avoid duplicate toys. Fewer toys will benefit your kids in many different ways. Kids will learn to be more creative and they learn to take greater care of their stuff. It results in a less-cluttered and healthier home!

313. Store and organize card games.

Your clutter demands energy and time. When your house or apartment is untidy and cluttered, it's harder to relax. A lot of unnecessary things distract us and make us confused. Clutter slows us down. Clutter comes with a price. The price is our peace. Declutter and organize your home and you will spend less time cleaning and maintaining item.

If your kids love card games, they should be properly organized. Why? If some cards have been lost, what's the point of keeping the game further? Ask yourself: Is this useful? So, get rid of useless card games. When you go to declutter kids' stuff you will find a lot of these items. So organize them clever. Here is a cheap and easy idea – You can use a soap organizer as a place to hold kid's card games!

314. A clever idea for big toys.

Toys everywhere. Large dolls, big plastic toys, toy trucks, and other big toys create a lot of our clutter. Keep big toys well organized and easily accessible by putting them in a plastic hamper! You can get your kids to pick up their toys. They only need a special place for their special items. It doesn't matter how much that special place costs. It could be an old basket as you can see. It's important to teach your kids to declutter their playroom.

315. Two life-changing decluttering hacks – reuse old toys!

"Inside of every problem lies an opportunity." – Robert Kiyosaki.

There is no doubt, finding a clever solution for organization of many toys can be very challenging. Keeping all toys in one place is difficult never ending battle. However, there are many solutions if you are willing to roll up your sleeves and face this problem. And you realize: every problem has a solution.

a. Instead of buying new storage containers, old Lego blocks can be used to corral small toys. Children can also keep their art supplies there.

b. The second idea is to use some of old wooden building blocks as modern design hooks! In this way, you get some interesting hooks to hang shawls, bags or keys. Thus, you will free up space in kid's room and make the most of old toys.

316. A storage chest.

Picture books, toys, and the other items tend to pile up over again. Consider buying a blanket chest or wicker chest. Anyway, you should purchase a low storage chest. In this way, you can store items that your kids use on a daily basis.

Kids playroom will be in order and you will finally be happy.

317. Declutter kids' clothes – basics.

When you go to declutter your kids' clothes, find some large boxes such as moving boxes, as well as a couple of garbage bags. You can also ask for empty boxes at your grocery store or local restaurant. Here is a simple question to keep in mind: Is this really useful? Here are some guidelines to get started decluttering of children's clothes:

a. **Toss, donate, or recycle.** Take everything out of the kids' closet. Have a trash bag on hand and toss unwanted pieces of clothing. Don't keep the pieces of clothes that need repair, unless you are planning to repair them.

b. **Clean up.** Then, wipe down the interior and shelves.

c. **What's the purpose?** Keep things that are in wearable condition. Throw away the items with stains or tiny holes.

d. **"To be, or not to be..."** Create a "maybe" box if you are unsure about some items. Make final decisions within a month.

e. **The best part.** Create your shopping list.

f. **Outgrown kids' clothes.** Carefully store outgrown kids' clothes if there are younger siblings that can wear hand-me-downs.

318. Organize outgrown kids' clothes.

After decluttering and organizing, you realize that you have a few boxes of outgrown kids' clothes. What will you do with all of those old kids' clothes? Is there anything better than see an organized wardrobe? Get this done today and you will be a happier in the evening. Ready, set, go!

Here are a few ideas to help you get rid of outgrown kids' clothes

Keep it for your future child. If you are going to have more kids, you can keep old clothes that are in wearable condition. Don' t save worn out or stained clothes. If you decide to keep clothes for your future child, there are a few tips to keep in mind.

- First and foremost, clean everything thoroughly.

- Never store your valuable clothes in the dry cleaning plastic bags.

- Loosely stack clothes into storage boxes or bags.

- Loosely pack shoes with clean tissue paper; it will help maintain their shape.

Donate. If you are not going to have any more children, consider donating. Remember – you can donate only good clothes. Donate kids' clothes that other people will love and want. Everything that is shabby, ripped or stained throw into a trash can!

Let it go. There are items of sentimental value for you. You might save these things for your future grandchild. But, think of it – they too will have many clothes for sure! Therefore, it's time to let go of past and make space for new memories.

319. Clutter-busting ideas for your little ones.

Remember – every solution must fit the child. Each and every storage solution has to be kid-friendly. Obviously, you can't use a storage such hanging rods or dresser drawer that are out of reach. Each and every piece of furniture, as well as storage space, must be suitable and accessible to small hands. Here are some useful ideas to tackle the storage problems:

- You can remove closet doors for easier access.

- Look for child-sized hangers.

- Then, you have to lower hanging rods.

- Use floor-level baskets and bins as much as you can.

- Consider building a comfy built-in window seat.

- Consider buying a small dresser with a few drawers.

- Don't forget – under the bed is a clever and useful storage spot. You can use under bed carts with wheels.

320. Display child's favorites.

A simple and inexpensive garment rack is always a great clutter-busting solution. You can turn kid's closet into a display for their favorites. There is an old rule – out of sight, out of mind. You can find a garment rack with extra storage on the bottom that could be utilized for kids' shoes and backpacks. Therefore, everything is transparent and accessible and it will make getting dressed quick and easy.

321. Reorganize and declutter room with wrought iron hooks.

Would it be great to have everyday items at your fingertips? You can use some wrought iron hooks to hold backpacks, jackets, baskets with handles, and other things. You can also hang the basket to hold small items such as craft supplies. Each child will be assigned a couple of hooks for holding her/his necessities. Lovely!

322. A catchall basket in a kids' room.

This is a clever idea to help your kids get organized in their room. Consider buying a large-sized decorative basket with a lid. Whenever your child leaves something lying around that doesn't belong in the kids' room, it goes into designated catchall basket. Put the basket into the corner of the room to save space. Clever!

323. Teach your little ones to be organized – multicolored drawers.

Teaching kids some good organizing habits can be tricky, but it's worth the effort. Is anything better than entering into kids' room and seeing a clean and organized space?

The multicolored drawers offer plenty of storage space for different kids' items such as socks, caps, underwear, etc. Your child will learn that underwear goes in green, caps in yellow, and so on. Easy!

PETS

Life hacks for a clutter-free pet's area

"Until one has loved an animal a part of one's soul remains unawakened." – Anatole France.

If your home is jammed with pet knickknacks and you can't manage it, it's time to relax. You always do your best, but things are getting out of control sometimes. No big deal!

You can learn how to keep pets' stuff organized. Organization of "pet zone" requires decluttering, cleaning, and sorting to make your space a calming haven. Let's get organized!

324. How to organize pet supplies?

Whether you have cats, dogs, hamster, or any other pets, these decluttering and purging tips will help you find a spot for pet supplies.

   a. Gather all of items in one place.

   b. Throw away damaged and broken items, as well as expired food.

   c. Donate unopened bags of food that your pet doesn't like to eat and items that are in good condition.

d. Now it's easy to organize the items that have left. There are a lot of storage and organization solutions and you can choose according to your personal preferences.

325. A clever organization for your beloved pet.

At the beginning, put like items together. For instance, gather items you need to walk your dog into one pile, bath accessories go in the second pile, etc. Create a station for each activity and your pet will get organized once and for all. Then, find a spot for each and every item.

It's wise to create a pet binder to keep important pet information well-organized and sorted. The information includes off-limit foods, allergies, anamnesis, the phone numbers of nearest veterinary clinics, pet passport, and so on.

326. Declutter and reorganize a walk station.

Position a dog walking station next to entrance. If you want to maintain uncluttered entryway, try to organize walking equipment. Keep leashes, treats, collars, doggy sacks and other items in a tote bag. Then, hang this bag on a hook and enjoy the new uncluttered look.

You can also store these items in a designated bin or another appropriate container. You can find these adorable containers online, too.

Prepare a home away bag for your dog by putting certain essentials. These are a water bottle, food bag, poop bags, chewy toys, and so on. It's great to have this home away bag on hand.

Catch clutter and reorganize your entryway!

327. Feed your fur friend.

For your pet, mealtime is one of the happiest moments of the day. Here're a few pointers to help you organize your pet.

a. It is important to designate a spot for bowls or pet feeders. Consider buying a pet food mat to keep the place neat and tidy.

b. Keep their dishes for food and water in an out-of-the-way spot so your pet will enjoy the meal without interruption. Choose dishes that suit the needs of your pet. Make sure that their food and water are easily accessible.

c. Toss unnecessary items and sort feeding supplies in order to keep them organized and easily accessible.

d. It's very important to keep pet food handy at feeding time. It should be right next to the feeding spot.

328. Keep pet food neatly organized.

Tired of wasting time searching for a bag with dry cat food you need? Your pantry is jammed with pet foods that are not sorted and organized?

- a. It's time to start throwing out the unwanted pet food. Gather up all products. Check out the expiration dates. Consider donating or giving away if you have a lot of food bags that your pet doesn't like. Only store what you will use.

- b. Now, group foods in a way that is logical to you.

- a. Designate a spot in your pantry for pet food. Add labels to jars for better organization results. Try your best to keep pet's food easily accessible and fresh. Store dry pet food in a cool and dry environment. Canned food should be stored in a dry environment (50-100 degrees F). If you prefer to buy food in bulk, you have to transfer dry food to an appropriate container. A clean metal container works well. Opened cans of dog/cat food should be stored in the refrigerator.

- b. Check the expiration dates periodically and keep the pantry tidy and clean.

329. Declutter and organize pet toys.

When you need pet's favorite toy or pillow, do you look through the whole house for it?

Our beloved pets have a lot of stuff. If you're stuck, start by setting small goals, one by one. When the time comes to declutter toys, stick to well-known basic rules to organize your pet supplies.

    a.   Gather all toys together and lay them on the ground. Sort them and discard the toys that are broken, old and useless.

    b.   It is important to store all pet toys in one place for better organization. Find suitable containers that don't take up too much space.

330. Adorable containers for pet toys.

If you decide to keep all pet toys in one designated place, you should purchase the appropriate storage bin or basket. Make your pets feel extra special by storing their toys in durable toy storage. After playing with your puppy or kitty, putting the toys back is as easy as ABC!

If you are switching the toys into new containers, try to maintain this uncluttered and beautiful look. Spend five minutes every evening putting the toys back where they belong and Voilà! Everything works in perfect order.

331. A special sleeping spot.

Cats and dogs love safe and quiet sleeping place. You can choose from different pet beds such as a built-in bed, plush bed, bag bed, etc. Find a suitable machine washable bed and maintain this area uncluttered and clean.

Remember – designate a spot for your fur friend in a quiet corner of your house. Your pet will spend a lot of time there. He/she will have a quiet sleeping spot and you will solve a problem with pet hair.

LAUNDRY ROOM

Let it shine!

Within the walls of our home, we try to live a balanced life. You do not have to have a large laundry room in order to be happy. You do not need to have a laundry room at all. All you need is a few simple and easy organizing tricks. Balance is the key to a happy home!

332. The plan for simplifying your laundry – basics.

If your laundry room is cluttered and you can't manage it, it's time to relax. You have too much laundry. So what? You always do your best, but things are getting out of control sometimes. No big deal!

You can learn how to keep your laundry room organized and more efficient. Here are a few tips:

a. **Declutter your laundry room.** Old and broken items, detergent bottles, ripped clothing… Out!

b. **Main purpose.** It is very important to define your laundry room. If you are able, use that room only for the task of laundry.

c. **Label it.** Label, at least, two laundry baskets: 1) by color and 2) by clothing type. You can label one more basket as "other". Ask all family members for help and you will appreciate it if they follow the specified rules. Declutter your life!

333. Declutter the laundry room – divide into zones.

Laundry room tends to fall into chaos without the right decluttering plan. Here's a plan to help you get well-organized. Divide your laundry room into zones: 1) an area for washer and dryer; 2) an area for laundry supplies; 3) drying zone; 4) laundry ironing and folding.

Focus on one area at a time to simplify your decluttering process and get organized.

334. Washer and dryer organization.

It's time to purchase pedestals for your washer and dryer. You can build them yourself, too. This easy project will make a pleasant laundry area.

Pedestal is a great spot for storing items in the laundry room. Let your imagination run wild and create the pedestal with drawers for an extra space storage. You can put baskets with laundry supplies into cubbies and save space significantly while keeping everything on hand. Lovely!

335. Space utilization – a smart organizer between washer and dryer.

You can also utilize space between washer and dryer by putting a laundry organizer. The laundry organizer takes vertical space and keeps your supplies within reach. There are a few handle drawers that slide smoothly, so you will be able to sort and group your laundry accessories.

Therefore, add storage and get everything organized. Improve your daily laundry routine!

336. A clever laundry concept – rolling laundry caddy.

There is one more amazing solution to utilize space between washer and dryer. Rolling laundry caddy keeps your laundry supplies perfectly in place. Its sturdy construction offers the reliability and overall ease of use.

The rolling laundry caddy provides you with a few shelves; therefore, you can group your items by categories. For example, the lowest shelf holds liquid and powder detergents, detergent capsules and tablets; the shelf in the middle holds fabric softeners and scent boosters; top shelf holds stain removers, bleach, etc. Anyhow, you will organize and sort your laundry accessories according to your personal preferences.

337. Get your cleaning supplies neatly organized.

Whatever you use liquid or powder detergent or you like to use homemade detergent, they can make clutter in your laundry room. Here are a few ideas to keep your cleaning supplies neat and tidy.

a. Your goal is to eliminate as much junk as possible, right? Check your cleaning supplies. Get rid of expired items and almost empty bags and bottles.

b. Realistically, how many laundry products do you need? Consider buying a detergent that works for all fabrics. Baking soda and vinegar are excellent homemade solutions for softening and protecting your clothes.

c. Use glass jars to keep track of your cleaning supplies. Remember – keep your detergents in a cool and dry place.

338. Behind the door – an over-the-door shoe organizer.

Do not underestimate the importance of a good organizer. However, you don't have to waste your hard-earned money on some expensive organizers. Turn a laundry door into extra storage space by hanging an over-the-door shoe organizer.

This versatile organizer can hold various types of things such as cleaners and tools. Therefore, you will keep them out of the way but visible.

Then, behind the door, you can designate a spot for essentials like a mop, broom, ironing tools, etc.

339. Think outside the jar.

a. Detergent tablets and pods, mini soaps and other small cleaning products are useful and innovative solutions, but they tend to be forgotten. You can store detergent capsules, pods and other small cleaning items in a glass candy jar.

b. Then, you can store your liquid detergent in a beverage dispenser. Simple but practical!

c. Remember – get rid of "just in case" items because these things take up so much space and weigh you down.

340. A great way to organize your cleaning supplies – under sink space.

Space under the sink is usually hard to get to and, therefore, it becomes forgotten over time. Space under the sink offers a lot of possibilities to store your laundry supplies.

a. Corral your detergents by using a metal caddy or a bucket and conceal it under your sink.

b. You can organize spray bottles by installing a tension rod under your sink.

c. Then, try to store garbage bags.

d. One of the most useful organizing solutions is a clear bin. Use a few clear bins to keep your detergents neatly organized. Go one step further and label your bins. Make cleanup a breeze!!

341. Organize your stain removal kit.

How many stain removers do you really need? Get rid of unwanted product and organize cute stain removal kit. Corral all stain removers in one basket. You can also use a rimmed tray. A Lazy Susan works well, too. It is important to keep your stain removal kit in an easy-to-access spot.

Then, put the basket or the tray under the sink. Now everything is well organized and easily accessible. Done!

342. How to use an old armoire to improve your laundry routine?

Avoid the hassle of rummaging through laundry room with an unfinished old armoire. Armoires fit into the unutilized space in a corner. Create a great laundry center in your basement or another suitable place.

a. The floor of the armoire makes a great spot for laundry bags.

b. Then, you can utilize the doors to hold cleaning items.

c. Use the shelves to keep detergent bags and bottles.

d. You can also use the top of armoire to store the items that are rarely used.

343. Great ideas to organize storage in your laundry room.

The laundry room is one of the most challenging rooms in your house. Therefore, the laundry room needs a systematic plan for organizing and decluttering.

If you want to keep all products and tools neatly organized, you should choose the right storage options.

Little plastic baskets. You can group like items by categories and designate a plastic basket for each category. They are great and cheap solutions for putting all items in their spots. Then, go one step further, find labels on the Internet, print them and put the label on each basket.

Bag laundry sorter. It is one of the best laundry organizers you will ever find. Your family will be able to divide all of their clothes among three separate hampers. This wheeled organizer is easy to use. When it comes time to wash clothes, empty out the hampers and that's it.

Once you've purchased a new organizer, you will wonder how you ever got along without it!

344. Organize your junk drawer.

If you have a junk drawer in your laundry room filled with clutter, it's time to organize it once and for all. You can tackle this task today. Ready set go!

a. Get four bags: "trash", "keep", "donate", and "other room". Bring all items together and divide them into one of these four bags.

b. Turn the drawer into functional storage for your essentials. Here are some of them: paper towels, tissues, light bulbs, extra soaps, cleaning wipes, and so on.

c. Use drawer dividers to reorganize your essentials, free up this useful storage space, and take control of your laundry room!

345. Adjustable laundry guard.

Cut clutter in your laundry room and utilize a top surface of your washer.

Install the laundry guard to keep your clothes on top of the washer, while providing an extra work surface in your laundry room. This innovative solution keeps clothes, especially small pieces like socks, from falling off. Clever!

346. The new concept for laundry room – shelves.

If your laundry room turns into a cramped space, here is a new inspiration and motivation for you!

You can use floating shelves to take advantage of space above a washer and dryer. This new custom look of your laundry offers a lot of possibilities to store all necessities (e.g. sewing kit, scissors, clothespins, laundry bags, etc.

You can divide these essentials into two main categories:

1) The items that are used most frequently go to the lowest shelves.

2) The items that are used rarely go to the highest shelves.

As you can see the shelves save space in the laundry room. Therefore, you can opt for waterproof wire shelves, too; they also offer many practical possibilities to streamline your laundry room.

347. Spend less time doing laundry – designated hampers.

Do you have just one or two cheap hampers? And your family fill them and do not sort laundry? Consider adding designated hampers. For example, label them like this: "colors", "white", "denim". Ask family members to separate clothes and group them by colors. Ask them to empty their pockets, too.

Then, try to hang your hampers and free up the floor space. Put this trick into practice and make your laundry day easier!

348. A few creative ways to make doing laundry easier.

a. **Rolling laundry basket dresser.** With this great asset, you can spend less time doing laundry for sure. Simply roll this basket dresser around your house and pick up the family's laundry. This mobile solution allows you to presort laundry easily and do laundry chore faster and better.

b. Labeled baskets. You can use cute laundry baskets assigned to each family member. Label them to save your time and give yourself a little peace of mind!

349. Instant laundry organization – a wall-hung cabinet.

Utilize all your wall space by hanging the cute cabinet to create a convenient laundry station. Cut clutter in your laundry room and find a spot for each and every item. Organizing your laundry routine is as easy as ABC! Here's how to achieve that.

a. Use the inside of your cabinet to organize laundry tools and accessories. Group items by frequency of use. The details matter, so consider adding wicker baskets for better organization.

b. Then, attach the iron holder to the side of your cabinet.

c. Next, beneath the iron, attach a clothes hanger that will hold ironed clothes and save space in your laundry room.

It does not sound just like a revolutionary idea, but you will build one small success on top of another small success. Afterwards, you can build a "mountain" of success. Say Goodbye to clutter and chaos and fall in love with order and beauty!

350. Perfect solutions for your drying zone – drying racks.

A drying rack is a perfect choice for clothes that need to be air-dried, such as button-down shirts.

a. **Folding drying rack.** It doesn't occupy a lot of space. Folding drying rack is adjustable and convenient solutions not only for the laundry room but also for the terrace.

b. **Rolling drying rack.** This is a great solution for your air drying and delicate clothes. This adjustable rack can be folded and easily rolled wherever you want.

c. **Versatile laundry center.** You can also find a rolling garment rack with shelves and get an extra storage with a portability feature.

351. DIY drying rack.

There is a great DIY hack that will improve your laundry chore. You can save space and time by installing a bath-towel holder on the underside of a shelf. Use hangers for extra space and enjoy this super-functional addition to your laundry room!

Of course, check the other DIY projects such as wooden ladder with hooks, projects with towel bars and clothes lines, etc. Be creative!

352. Fold away ironing board.

You can turn the most unorganized space in the house into the peaceful haven.

Your ironing board can take up a lot of space and your laundry room looks cluttered. However difficult decluttering task may seem, there is a simple solution. You can save your space by building the fold away ironing board instead. Get a spotless and beautiful laundry room!

353. An ingenious idea – pull out folding table.

It will free up space in your laundry room, while providing you with a useful surface for folding laundry. It is more convenient to use than a traditional table for quick touch-ups for your clothes. You will be surprised how pleasant laundry can be when space is user-friendly.

GARAGE

Let's get organized!

Do you need a convenient and efficient place to work? Do you need an extra storage in a limited garage space?

One day you realize – your garage is jammed with stuff and you forgot of your passion and dreams because of your hectic lifestyle. There are a lot of easy and practical solutions to get your garage neat and tidy. Take back your garage, follow your passion and enjoy your home to the fullest!

354. Declutter your garage – tackle this task over the weekend.

If your garage is a messy place filled with unnecessary items, it's time to take back this valuable space.

The garage is usually jammed with tools, equipment, automotive gear, seasonal supplies, etc. Unfortunately, the garage is holding area for the clutter from the house, too. However, you have to solve this clutter problem sooner or later.

You can apply some of these ideas and find what suits your usage level.

One of the best methods to declutter garage is to divide this space into zones. For example, automotive, tools, gardening, and storage. If you find some items that don't fit into one of these designated "zones", consider donating or tossing them. It's just that simple!

355. Focus on one area at a time.

Set the mood with your favorite music and get to work! Focus on one area at a time. Try to break down the job into a few small manageable tasks and avoid discouragement and tiredness.

a. Bring all items together. Consider tossing, selling or donating unwanted items. Get rid of things "just in case", too.

b. The rest of items that you have decided to keep, group by categories.

c. Use large totes because they can hold many things.

d. Designate an empty bin for the clutter from your house. From time to time, you should empty this bin and maintain this clutter-free environment.

356. How to keep all of your gardening tools neat and tidy?

If you are tired of seeing the clutter in your garage or a shed and waste time looking for tools, it's time to solve this problem. There is no doubt – clutter can really influence the way you work. The well-organized tools will save you time and energy. Here're simple hacks for decluttering the garden shed.

1) Take out all of you gardening tools that you have in the garage. Check out each individual tool. Clean out everything.

2) Create two piles: 1) items that you want to keep, and 2) items that you need to get rid of. Get rid of everything that is broken and useless. That's simply trash.

3) Reorganize your tools. For example: keep frequently used tools close at hand using the hooks. Use a pegboard to hang small tools. Use an old wooden palette for larger tools. Find a convenient place to store each and every tool and you will tackle this task over the weekend.

357. Creative organization solutions – install shelving.

Get more storage space in your garage by installing vertical shelving systems. Free up floor space and organize all items by function.

Sturdy wire racks can hold almost anything, but you can choose from the other materials such as wood, metal or plastic. It depends on your personal needs. Use different containers to group all items by categories and keep your garage neatly organized. You can use small bins for items such as flashlights, rolls of adhesive, and so on. From now onwards, you will see everything!

358. Utilize the garage ceiling.

Whether you have a small or large garage, there is probably a lot of space you aren't using such as the ceilings. You can hang bikes and free up the floor space.

Then, you can storage containers to the ceiling by using wood boards and elbow grease. This space-saving product will take some time but the advantages are significant.

359. Hang a pegboard in your garage.

Classic pegboard (perforated hardboard) is one of the most effective ways to organize your tools and accessories in the garage. This space-saving storage solution is easy to install, cheap and practical. Of course, you should follow manufacturer's instruction in order to reduce the risk of personal injury. Utilize a vertical space in your garage and make your tools more visible.

360. A creative storage idea – old school lockers.

Here is an amazing and inexpensive storage solution for you – find old school lockers. You can find them online, paint them and assign one to each family member.

Our clutter defines a part of us as a person. For example, if you love collectibles, these things reflect your passion. Anyway, most of these things end in your garage. One day you realize – your garage is jammed with stuff and you forgot of your passion and dreams because of your hectic lifestyle.

These personalized lockers offer you the possibility to organize your stuff. Clever!

361. A practical solution – drawers in your garage.

Drawers are always simple but practical garage storage for your necessities.

First and foremost, you should identify all of your needs. How many items are you planning to keep in your drawers? You can build DIY sturdy drawers or reuse an old dresser.

Clean some shoe boxes and put them into your drawers to take your task to the next level.

362. A space-saving solution – workbench.

Do you need a convenient and efficient place to work? Do you need an extra work surface in a limited space? A workbench is a space-saving solution for your garage.

    a. You can reuse a spare chest of drawers.

    b. The second solution is to build your own sturdy workbench to fit your workshop and your needs. There are lots of different designs of the workbench. You can choose from folding workbench, workbench with drawers and shelves for tool storage, modular workbench, and so on.

363. Utilize every bit of space – corner shelves.

Clear the clutter and utilize every unused nook in your garage. Build the corner shelves and organize all small items in your garage. These shelves will provide you with an easy access to everything.

    a. First and foremost, get rid of unwanted stuff!

    b. After that, you can manage what you own in your garage. Designate a spot for every item.

    c. If you can't find a spot for certain item, it means – toss or remove to another location in your house.

    d. Then, display small items on your corner shelves and enjoy clutter-free garage!

Utilize every bit of space in your garage!

364. A simple idea to organize gardening tools.

Use leftover PVC pipes to create a tool holder.

1) First, cut the pieces of pipes to length at an angle on the bandsaw.

2) Then, drill the hole into each of them. Attach them to the wall.

3) Designate a certain pipe for certain group of items. Arrange your gardening tools. Therefore, you can always find them quickly and easily.

And from now on, when you want to find some tool, you will always know where it is.

365. Keep balls neat and tidy.

If you store outdoor toys and sport equipment in your garage, and the garage is jammed with clutter, it's time to handle the problem. Do not settle with living in a messy environment. It's important not to limit yourself.

You can utilize space between the studs. You can use bungee cords to store balls. So install ball holder and keep your balls organized with the attached bungee cords.

Thank you for reading, If you have enjoyed this book, please take a few seconds to leave feedback for book on Amazon and get a free Kindle copy through the Kindle Matchbook Program.

18939188R00123

Printed in Great Britain
by Amazon